Security-Driven Software Development

Learn to analyze and mitigate risks in your software projects

Aspen Olmsted

Security-Driven Software Development

Group Product Manager: Kunal Sawant

Publishing Product Manager: Akash Sharma

Book Project Manager: Manisha Singh

Senior Editor: Kinnari Chohan

Technical Editor: Vidhisha Patidar

Copy Editor: Safis Editing

Indexer: Hemangini Bari

Production Designer: Joshua Misquitta

DevRel Marketing Coordinator: Sonia Chauhan

First published: February 2024

Production reference: 1230224

Published by Packt Publishing Ltd.

Grosvenor House

11 St Paul's Square

Birmingham

B3 1RB, UK

ISBN 978-1-83546-283-6

www.packtpub.com

To my family, Freya, Seamus, and Kirsten.
I appreciate how you always believe in me.

Contributors

About the author

Aspen Olmsted is an associate professor and program director at Wentworth Institute of Technology in the computer science department. He obtained a Ph.D. in computer science and engineering from the University of South Carolina. Before his academic career, he was CEO of Alliance Software Corporation. Alliance Software developed N-Tier enterprise applications for the performing arts and humanities market. Dr. Olmsted's research focus is on the development of algorithms and architectures for distributed enterprise solutions that can guarantee security and correctness while maintaining high availability. Aspen mentors over a dozen graduate and undergraduate students in his Secure Data Engineering Lab each year.

About the reviewer

Alon Hillel-Tuch, a seasoned technical founder, established RocketHub, a notable financial services platform recognized as a Department of State Global Partner in 2015. His expertise extends to being Managing Partner of an early-stage venture fund focused on govtech, infrastructure, and frontier technologies. Renowned for his insights into startup investment structures, Alon has testified twice before the U.S. Congress on innovation, regulation, and digital security, and spearheaded FINRA's Capital Market Series XVII. He is a founding board member of the Forbes Technology Council and the Crowdfunding Professional Association. Alon holds an M.Sc. in Negotiation and Conflict Resolution from Columbia University and an M.Sc. in Cybersecurity from New York University.

Table of Contents

Part 1: Modeling a Secure Application

1

Security Principles   3

2

Designing a Secure Functional Model   15

Part 2: Mitigating Risks in Implementation

7

Authentication and Authorization   101

8

Input Validation and Sanitization   117

9

Standard Web Application Vulnerabilities   129

Part 3: Security Validation

Preface

This book explores the foundations of software security. We'll consider important software vulnerabilities and attacks that exploit them – such as buffer overflows, SQL injection, and session hijacking – and defenses that prevent or mitigate these attacks, including advanced testing and program analysis techniques. Importantly, we'll take a "build security in" mentality, considering techniques at each phase of the development cycle that can be used to strengthen the security of software systems.

Who this book is for

This book is for anyone who can program in any programming language and wants to learn how to build more secure and robust software.

What this book covers

Chapter 1, Security Principles and Procedures, gives us a foundation of some standard principles and procedures used in secure software development.

Chapter 2, Designing a Secure Functional Model, teaches us how to specify what our software should do and what should be true while the software is executing.

Chapter 3, Designing a Secure Object Model, helps us to identify the objects and structures we will use in our software application.

Chapter 4, Designing a Secure Dynamic Model, helps us think about how the objects in our programs will interact with each other.

Chapter 5, Designing a Secure System Model, explores how we partition our application into subsystems and helps us think about how those partitions can communicate securely.

Chapter 6, Threat Modeling, is where we model the risks to our software and start to think about the mitigations we can deploy to reduce those risks.

Chapter 7, Authentication and Authorization, explores utilizing authentication and authorization to mitigate risks identified in our threat models.

Chapter 8, Input Validation and Sanitization, explores input validation and sanitization to mitigate risks identified in our threat models.

Chapter 9, Standard Web Application Vulnerabilities, discusses the many common vulnerabilities that are found in web applications.

Chapter 10, Database Security, takes a deep dive into databases and the risks and mitigations we can use while our software interacts with the database.

Chapter 11, Unit Testing, looks at ensuring our software performs the functions and meets the non-functional requirements we specified earlier in our model on small unit levels.

Chapter 12, Regression Testing, looks at ensuring our software performs the functions and meets the non-functional requirements we specified earlier in our model as code is changed.

Chapter 13, Integration Testing, looks at ensuring our software performs the functions and meets the non-functional requirements we specified earlier in our model as we put the different partitions and subsystems together.

Chapter 14, Penetration Testing, considers how we can discover vulnerabilities that slipped through despite our earlier hard work modeling, planning, and testing.

To get the most out of this book

- You should be able to code in a programming language.

- You should have a software project you want to develop.

- You should be able to read code in other languages and be able to decipher the gist of the code.

- You should be able to install or utilize a cloud-based UML tool.

Conventions used

There are a number of text conventions used throughout this book.

`Code in text`: Indicates code words in text, database table names, folder names, filenames, file extensions, pathnames, dummy URLs, user input, and Twitter handles. Here is an example: "Mount the downloaded `WebStorm-10*.dmg` disk image file as another disk in your system."

A block of code is set as follows:

```
public function testInvalidNoLowerCasePassword() {
  $person = new Person('testUser@aol.com');
  $this->assertFalse($person->create_login('UPPERCASE1!'));
  $this->assertNull($person->getPassword());
}
```

Any command-line input or output is written as follows:

```
ls -l|grep "cats"
```

> **Tips or important notes**
> Appear like this.

Get in touch

Feedback from our readers is always welcome.

General feedback: If you have questions about any aspect of this book, email us at `customercare@ packtpub.com` and mention the book title in the subject of your message.

Errata: Although we have taken every care to ensure the accuracy of our content, mistakes do happen. If you have found a mistake in this book, we would be grateful if you would report this to us. Please visit `www.packtpub.com/support/errata` and fill in the form.

Piracy: If you come across any illegal copies of our works in any form on the internet, we would be grateful if you would provide us with the location address or website name. Please contact us at `copyright@packt.com` with a link to the material.

If you are interested in becoming an author: If there is a topic that you have expertise in and you are interested in either writing or contributing to a book, please visit `authors.packtpub.com`.

Share your thoughts

Once you've read *Security-Driven Software Development*, we'd love to hear your thoughts! Scan the QR code below to go straight to the Amazon review page for this book and share your feedback.

`https://packt.link/r/1835462839`

Your review is important to us and the tech community and will help us make sure we're delivering excellent quality content.

Download a free PDF copy of this book

Thanks for purchasing this book!

Do you like to read on the go but are unable to carry your print books everywhere?

Is your eBook purchase not compatible with the device of your choice?

Don't worry, now with every Packt book you get a DRM-free PDF version of that book at no cost.

Read anywhere, any place, on any device. Search, copy, and paste code from your favorite technical books directly into your application.

The perks don't stop there, you can get exclusive access to discounts, newsletters, and great free content in your inbox daily

Follow these simple steps to get the benefits:

1. Scan the QR code or visit the link below

https://packt.link/free-ebook/9781835462836

2. Submit your proof of purchase
3. That's it! We'll send your free PDF and other benefits to your email directly

Part 1: Modeling a Secure Application

The first part of this book drills into modeling a secure application so we can identify the risks to our application before we start our implementation. The process is iterative, so we'll revisit previous models as we add knowledge about new models.

This part has the following chapters:

- *Chapter 1, Security Principles and Procedures*
- *Chapter 2, Designing a Secure Functional Model*
- *Chapter 3, Designing a Secure Object Model*
- *Chapter 4, Designing a Secure Dynamic Model*
- *Chapter 5, Designing a Secure System Model*
- *Chapter 6, Threat Modeling*

1

Security Principles

Software development security principles are guidelines and best practices that help ensure the security of software applications throughout their development life cycle. These principles are essential for protecting sensitive data, preventing security breaches, and maintaining users' trust.

In this chapter, we're going to cover security principles by looking at the following main topics:

- What could go wrong?
- Principles
- Open Web Application Security Project
- NIST's Secure Software Development Framework
- MITRE frameworks
- Software development life cycles
- Microsoft's Security Development Lifecycle
- Confidentiality, integrity, and availability in software development

The goal of the chapter is to give you a good foundation of some secure software terminology along with an understanding of the current state of the practice. We will reference the topics of this chapter in future chapters.

What could go wrong?

Over the past few decades, there have been tens of thousands of successful malicious software security attacks. These include a data attack that affected approximately 40 million Target customers, the Facebook-Cambridge Analytica scandal in 2018, which involved unauthorized access to user data through a third-party app's API, and an XSS scripting attack that, within 20 hours, infected over one million Myspace profiles.

Hundreds of thousands of unintended user mistakes are due to poorly designed or implemented software. These mistakes often go unreported, even though the software or experiment may fail, or humans are harmed. Some examples include NASA's Mars Climate Orbiter, where the spacecraft's navigation software used metric units, while ground control provided data in imperial units. This mismatch resulted in incorrect calculations, causing the orbiter to approach Mars at too low an altitude, ultimately leading to its failure. Another example is Ariane 5's flight 501, where the rocket's inertial reference system software failed due to a data conversion error. The software was reused from the previous Ariane 4 model but proved incompatible with the higher velocity of Ariane 5. This led to a catastrophic failure within 40 seconds of liftoff.

The most well-known error from poorly designed software was the Therac-25 radiation therapy machine, where the software and hardware design flaws in the Therac-25 medical device led to patients receiving massive overdoses of radiation. The software allowed for race conditions, and insufficient testing failed to catch critical errors in the system.

Unintended programmer mistakes often lead to both malicious and unintended software failures. An excellent example is when a programming mistake in the OpenSSL cryptographic software led to the Heartbleed bug. This flaw allowed attackers to read sensitive data from the memory of thousands of web servers, compromising user privacy.

Principles

Software security principles are fundamental guidelines and best practices that help design, develop, and maintain secure software systems. These principles aim to protect software applications and their data from a wide range of threats and vulnerabilities. Here are some fundamental software security principles:

- **Least privilege**: Give individuals or processes only the minimum access and permissions they need to perform their tasks. This principle reduces the potential for unauthorized access or abuse of privileges.

- **Defense in depth**: Implement multiple security controls and safeguards layers rather than relying solely on a single security measure. This approach helps to mitigate risks and reduce the impact of security breaches.

- **Fail-safe defaults**: Configure systems and applications to operate securely by default. Fail-safe defaults mean that if a configuration or access control is not explicitly defined, it should be denied or disabled.

- **Input validation**: Validate and sanitize all user inputs to prevent injection attacks, such as **SQL injection** and **cross-site scripting** (**XSS**). Input validation helps ensure that data is safe before it's processed.

- **Output encoding**: Encode data before it is displayed to users. This encoding prevents attacks such as XSS by ensuring potentially malicious input is treated as data, not code.

- **Secure data storage**: Use strong encryption and access controls to protect sensitive data at rest. This principle includes encrypting data in databases, files, and other storage locations.

- **Authentication and authorization**: Implement robust authentication mechanisms to verify the identity of users and authorization controls to ensure that users can access only the resources and functionality they are allowed to.

- **Session management**: Properly manage and secure user sessions to prevent session fixation, session hijacking, and other session-related attacks.

- **Secure communication**: Use secure protocols such as HTTPS to protect data transmitted between clients and servers.

- **Error handling**: Implement appropriate error handling and reporting mechanisms to provide minimal information to users while logging detailed error messages for administrators.

- **Secure dependencies**: Regularly update and patch all software components and libraries to address known vulnerabilities. Ensure that third-party dependencies are secure and up to date.

- **Security testing**: Conduct thorough security testing, including code reviews, penetration testing, and vulnerability scanning, to identify and remediate security issues in the software.

- **Security training and awareness**: Promote security awareness among developers, users, and administrators and provide training to ensure they understand and follow security best practices.

- **Incident response**: Develop a plan to respond to security breaches and minimize their impact effectively.

- **Security by design**: Consider security from the initial stages of software design and architecture rather than attempting to bolt security onto a finished product.

- **Secure development life cycle**: Implement a secure **software development life cycle (SDLC)** incorporating security activities at each development phase, from requirements to deployment.

- **Threat modeling**: Identify and assess potential threats and vulnerabilities specific to your application, allowing you to address security issues proactively.

These principles provide a foundation for building and maintaining secure software applications. They should be integrated into the development process and adapted to each application's specific requirements and threat landscape. By following these principles, software developers and organizations can reduce the risk of security breaches and protect their applications and users. Next, we will look at a few specific frameworks to see how they tackle these important software security principles.

Open Web Application Security Project

When considering software security principles, you must reference **Open Web Application Security Project (OWASP)** terminology. OWASP is an online community and organization that focuses on web application security. OWASP is known for its extensive collection of resources and tools related to web application security, which are freely available to the public. The primary goal of OWASP is to improve software security by providing knowledge and tools that help organizations and individuals develop and maintain secure web applications.

Some of the critical activities and resources associated with OWASP include the following:

- **Top 10**: This is a regularly updated list of the top 10 most critical web application security risks. It serves as a guide for developers and organizations to prioritize their security efforts.

- **Projects**: OWASP sponsors and supports various open source projects related to web application security. These projects cover various security topics, including secure coding, vulnerability scanning, and penetration testing.

- **Web application security testing**: OWASP offers guidelines, tools, and resources for testing the security of web applications, helping organizations identify and address vulnerabilities.

- **Cheat sheets**: These practical guides and checklists provide developers and security professionals with best practices and recommendations for secure coding and testing.

- **Web security testing guide**: This comprehensive guide provides information on conducting security assessments and testing web applications for vulnerabilities.

- **AppSensor**: This is a project that focuses on the detection and response to application-level attacks, guiding on implementing real-time application security monitoring.

- **Chapters and conferences**: OWASP has local chapters and organizes events and conferences worldwide, facilitating the exchange of knowledge and best practices in web application security.

- **Software Assurance Maturity Model (SAAM)**: SAAM is a framework for organizations to evaluate and improve their software security practices.

OWASP's work is widely respected in the cybersecurity community, and its resources are commonly used by developers, security professionals, and organizations to enhance the security of web applications. OWASP operates on a community-driven and open source philosophy, making its resources and knowledge accessible to everyone interested in web application security.

NIST's Secure Software Development Framework

The **National Institute of Standards and Technology (NIST)** released various guidelines and frameworks for secure software development. One of the critical resources NIST provides is the NIST **Secure Software Development Framework (SSDF)**, designed to help organizations enhance the security of their software development processes. Here's an overview of the NIST SSDF:

- **Secure software development guidelines**: NIST's SSDF provides guidance on secure software development practices. It covers many topics, including requirements analysis, design, coding, testing, deployment, and maintenance, with a strong focus on security.

- **Secure software development principles:** The framework promotes fundamental security principles and best practices to be integrated into every phase of the software development life cycle. These principles include secure coding, security testing, threat modeling, and secure software architecture.

- **Security standards and references:** NIST's SSDF references various security standards, guidelines, and resources that can help organizations implement secure software development practices effectively. SSDF includes NIST Special Publications, industry standards, and other authoritative sources.

- **Security risk management:** The framework emphasizes the importance of risk management throughout the software development process. It encourages organizations to identify, assess, and mitigate security risks associated with their software projects.

- **Integration with existing processes:** NIST's SSDF is designed to be flexible and adaptable. Organizations can integrate its guidance and recommendations into their software development processes, including Agile and DevOps methodologies.

- **Security training and awareness:** The framework underscores the significance of training and raising awareness among developers, testers, and other stakeholders regarding secure coding practices and the implications of security vulnerabilities.

- **Security metrics and measurement:** NIST's SSDF encourages organizations to define and track security metrics to assess the effectiveness of their secure software development initiatives. Metrics can help identify areas for improvement and evaluate the impact of security measures.

- **Secure SDLC:** NIST's SSDF promotes incorporating security activities into the entire SDLC, from initial planning and requirements to post-deployment maintenance and monitoring.

- **Continuous improvement:** The framework emphasizes continuous improvement by learning from security incidents, security assessments, and feedback from the development process. It encourages organizations to adapt and refine their practices over time.

NIST's SSDF is a valuable resource for organizations seeking to improve the security of their software development processes. It provides a structured approach to integrating security considerations into every phase of the SDLC, ultimately leading to more robust and secure software applications.

> **Note**
> Please refer to official NIST publications and resources to get the latest and most detailed information on NIST's SSDF.

MITRE frameworks

MITRE Corporation is a not-for-profit organization that operates **Federally Funded Research and Development Centers (FFRDCs)** in the United States. One of MITRE's key contributions to software security is the development and maintenance of the **Common Weakness Enumeration (CWE)** and **Common Vulnerabilities and Exposures (CVE)** standards:

1. **CWE:**

- **Purpose**: CWE is a community-developed dictionary of common software weaknesses that can lead to security vulnerabilities. It provides a standardized way to identify, describe, and categorize software weaknesses.

- **Use cases**: Developers, security professionals, and researchers use CWE to identify and mitigate vulnerabilities during the SDLC. It aids in improving the security of software by providing a common language for discussing and addressing weaknesses.

2. **CVE:**

- **Purpose**: CVE is a standardized identifier system for publicly known security vulnerabilities. Each CVE entry includes a unique identifier, a description of the vulnerability, and references to resources that provide additional information.

- **Use cases**: CVE is widely used in the cybersecurity community for tracking and referencing vulnerabilities. Security researchers, vendors, and organizations use CVE identifiers to communicate about specific security issues consistently.

3. **MITRE ATT&CK framework:**

- **Purpose**: The MITRE **Adversarial Tactics, Techniques, and Common Knowledge (ATT&CK)** framework is a knowledge base that describes the actions and behaviors of cyber adversaries. It provides a comprehensive view of adversaries' various tactics and techniques to achieve their objectives.

- **Use cases**: Security professionals, threat hunters, and incident responders use the ATT&CK framework to enhance their understanding of cyber threats and to improve defenses. It helps organizations assess their security postures and responses to different adversary behaviors.

MITRE's contributions to software security, mainly through CWE and CVE, play a crucial role in standardizing the identification and communication of vulnerabilities. These efforts contribute to a more secure and resilient software ecosystem by providing a common foundation for addressing weaknesses and sharing information about security threats and exposures.

Software development lifecycles

SDLCs are systematic processes or methodologies that software development teams use to plan, design, build, test, deploy, and maintain software applications. These life cycles help ensure that software projects are completed efficiently, on time, and within budget while meeting the specified requirements and maintaining high quality. There are several different SDLC models, and the choice of which one to use depends on the project's needs and requirements. Here are some of the most common SDLC models:

- **Waterfall model**: The Waterfall model is a sequential set of steps involved in software development. It divides the project into distinct phases: requirements, design, implementation, testing, deployment, and maintenance. Each phase must be completed before the next one begins, and it is challenging to make changes after a phase is complete. It is well-suited for projects with well-defined requirements that are unlikely to change.

- **Agile model**: Agile is an iterative and incremental software development approach focusing on flexibility and customer collaboration. It breaks the project into smaller, manageable iterations, often called sprints. Requirements and solutions evolve through the collaborative effort of self-organizing, cross-functional teams. It is well-suited for projects with evolving or unclear requirements.

- **Scrum**: Scrum is a specific framework within the Agile methodology that provides a set of roles, ceremonies, and artifacts for managing work. It emphasizes regular, time-boxed meetings and the continuous delivery of a potentially shippable product increment. Scrum teams work in short cycles, typically two to four weeks, called sprints.

- **Kanban**: Kanban is another Agile approach that visualizes the workflow and manages work in progress. It uses a Kanban board to represent tasks or user stories as cards that move through columns representing different stages of development. Teams pull work from a backlog as capacity allows.

- **Iterative model**: The Iterative model involves repeating cycles (iterations) of development, where a subset of the software's features is developed and tested in each iteration. It allows for changes and improvements to be made during each iteration. It is well-suited for projects that can benefit from ongoing refinement and feedback.

- **Spiral model**: The Spiral model is a combination of the Waterfall model with iterative and risk-driven development. It involves repeated planning cycles, risk analysis, engineering, and testing. It is well-suited for large and complex projects where risk management is a priority.

- **DevOps**: DevOps is not a traditional SDLC but a set of practices emphasizing close collaboration between development and operations teams. It aims to automate the deployment and operations of software to improve the speed and reliability of software delivery.

- **V-Model (Validation and Verification model)**: The V-Model is an extension of the Waterfall model, emphasizing the relationship between each development phase and its corresponding testing phase. Each development phase has a corresponding testing phase, resulting in a V-shaped diagram.

- **Rapid application development (RAD)**: RAD is an incremental, fast-paced SDLC model focusing on rapid prototyping and quick feedback. It is well-suited for projects that require a fast time-to-market.

- **Big Bang model**: The Big Bang model is an informal and unstructured approach where developers start coding without a specific plan or methodology. It is rarely used for large or critical projects but may be used for small, experimental projects.

The choice of which SDLC model to use depends on project requirements, the development team's experience, project size, budget, and the need for flexibility or predictability. Many organizations also customize or combine these models to create a hybrid SDLC that best suits their needs. Independent of the model used, the models used in this book are still developing. The scope of the model's work is different, but all SDLC models will still support and benefit from the methodology described in this book.

Microsoft's Security Development Lifecycle

The Microsoft **Security Development Lifecycle** (**SDL**) is a set of practices and guidelines that Microsoft has developed and implemented to improve the security of its software products. The SDL is designed to ensure that security is integral to the software development process from the beginning. It includes a set of best practices, tools, and processes that help identify and address security vulnerabilities at all stages of software development. Here are some critical aspects of the Microsoft SDL:

- **Training and education**: The SDL emphasizes training and education for developers and other stakeholders to raise awareness of security issues and best practices. The training includes secure coding training and security awareness programs.

- **Threat modeling**: One of the critical elements of the SDL is threat modeling, which involves identifying potential threats and vulnerabilities in the design and architecture of the software. By understanding these threats early in the development process, security measures can be implemented to mitigate them.

- **Static analysis tools**: Microsoft uses static code analysis tools to automatically scan code for security vulnerabilities. These tools can help detect buffer overflows, SQL injection, and other standard security problems.

- **Security code reviews**: Manual code reviews are essential to the SDL. Developers and security experts review code to identify security issues that automated tools might miss.

- **Penetration testing**: Penetration testing is conducted to identify vulnerabilities and weaknesses in the software. It involves trying to exploit the software in a controlled manner to discover potential security flaws.

- **Security design and review**: The SDL includes security design reviews to assess the software's architecture and design security. Any issues identified during these reviews are addressed before implementation.

- **Security testing**: Comprehensive security testing is performed throughout development to find and remediate vulnerabilities. This testing includes **dynamic application security testing**

(**DAST**) and fuzz testing. We will discuss automated testing more in *Chapters 11* to *14*, where we discuss software valuation and penetration testing.

- **Incident response planning**: The SDL includes planning for security incident response. This planning ensures the development team is prepared to respond effectively to security incidents or breaches.

- **Compliance and privacy**: The SDL considers regulatory compliance and privacy requirements. This process helps ensure that Microsoft's software products meet legal and privacy standards.

- **Security updates and patching**: Microsoft is committed to providing timely security updates and patches for its products. This process is a crucial aspect of maintaining software security post-release.

- **Continuous improvement**: The SDL is a continuously evolving process. Microsoft incorporates feedback and lessons learned into each iteration of the SDL to improve security practices.

Microsoft's adoption of the SDL has not only improved the security of its software products but has also positively influenced the software development industry as a whole. Microsoft has made many of its SDL resources and tools available to the public, allowing other organizations to implement similar practices and enhance the security of their software development processes. The process described in this book aims to be closer to the source code and cover more lines of code than the Microsoft model.

Confidentiality, integrity, and availability

CIA is an acronym representing the core principles of information security: **confidentiality, integrity, and availability**. These principles are fundamental to designing and implementing secure systems and are often called the **CIA triad**:

- **Confidentiality** ensures that information is only accessible to those with authorized permissions. Software security involves encryption, access controls, and user authentication to protect sensitive data from unauthorized access.

- **Integrity** ensures that information remains accurate and unaltered during storage, processing, or transmission. In software security, techniques such as data validation, checksums, digital signatures, and version control are used to maintain data and software integrity.

- **Availability** ensures that information and resources are available and accessible when needed. Software security involves measures to prevent and mitigate disruptions, such as redundancy, failover systems, and robust backup procedures, to ensure that software and data are available despite attacks or failures.

These principles guide the development of security policies, practices, and technologies to protect against various threats, including unauthorized access, data breaches, and service disruptions. Security professionals and developers often use the CIA triad as a framework to assess and enhance the security posture of software systems. Many of the historical software security issues discussed in the *What can go wrong?* section earlier all point back to these three categories of issues.

Summary

This chapter introduced secure software development principles. We looked at some organizations supporting the secure software development process, including OWASP and NIST. We also discussed the standard principles recognized by most secure developers. Next, we examined differences in different software development models and realized that the methodology presented in this book will work with all the different life cycles, independent of which are used. Lastly, we explored the Microsoft SDL and compared the approach presented in this book.

In the next chapter, we will look at building a more extensive example project based on what we have learned.

Self-assessment questions

1. What is the primary purpose of the "fail securely" principle?

    A. To avoid using third-party libraries

    B. To ensure that the application never experiences failures

    C. To immediately shut down the application in case of any issue

    D. To gracefully handle failures while maintaining security measures

2. What does the "divide and conquer" principle in secure design suggest?

    A. Security measures should be concentrated in a single layer for easier management

    B. Security tasks should be assigned to separate teams for better efficiency

    C. Complex problems should be divided into smaller, manageable components

    D. The application's features should be divided between different development teams

3. Why does the principle of "minimize attack surface" suggest that applications should have fewer exposed entry points?

    A. To reduce the potential points of vulnerability and attack

    B. To increase the application's processing speed

    C. To enhance the user experience

    D. To limit the number of users who can access the application

4. The "security by design" principle emphasizes that security measures should be what?

    A. An afterthought in the development process

    B. Integrated into the design and architecture from the beginning

    C. Added only in the final stages of development

    D. Implemented separately from the main application components

5. Which organization creates and maintains the OWASP Top Ten list of secure design principles?

    A. NIST

    B. World Wide Web Consortium (W3C)

    C. Internet Engineering Task Force (IETF)

    D. OWASP

6. "Validation and encoding" is a secure design principle that helps prevent what?

    A. Social engineering attacks

    B. Data loss due to hardware failure

    C. Physical breaches

    D. Injection attacks

7. In the context of secure design, what does the "privacy protection" principle focus on?

    A. Ensuring that user data is collected and stored without restrictions

    B. Preventing users from sharing personal information

    C. Encrypting all communication between users and the application

    D. Protecting sensitive user information from unauthorized access and disclosure

8. What does the "least common mechanism" principle suggest?

    A. The least commonly used authentication methods should be employed

    B. Sharing mechanisms across different components should be avoided to limit risk

    C. Common mechanisms should be used to increase efficiency

    D. Users should be given the least common features to minimize complexity

9. What does the "keep security simple and practical" principle recommend?

    A. Relying solely on user education for security awareness

    B. Implementing all available security features, regardless of complexity

    C. Keeping security solutions straightforward and easy to understand

    D. Using complex security measures to deter attackers.

10. "Abuse cases" in secure design involve identifying potential what?

    A. Business opportunities

    B. User interface improvements

    C. Performance bottlenecks

    D. Misuse scenarios and security threats

Answers

1. D
2. C
3. A
4. B
5. D
6. D
7. D
8. B
9. C
10. D

2

Designing a Secure Functional Model

Designing a secure, functional model is crucial in building a secure software application. The functional model defines how the application's features and functionalities work together while considering security.

In this chapter, we're going to cover designing a secure functional model by looking at the following main topics:

- Requirements gathering and specification
- Non-functional requirements and security
- Capturing scenarios
- Textual use cases and misuse cases
- Graphical use cases and misuse cases
- Example enterprise secure functional model

The goal of this chapter is to develop the tools and techniques to formally specify what needs to be built and what should be true when the software is running.

Requirements gathering and specification

Software requirements can be broadly categorized into three main types: functional, non-functional, and constraints. These three categories help define what the software needs to do, how it should perform, and any limitations or restrictions that must be considered:

- **Functional requirements**: Functional requirements specify what the software system should do regarding its features and capabilities. These requirements describe the system's behavior and functionality, often in the form of use cases or user stories. Functional requirements answer questions such as "*What does the software need to accomplish?*" They can include features, user interactions, and data processing tasks. Examples of functional requirements include the following:

- **User authentication**: Users must be able to create accounts, log in, and reset passwords. User authentication is an example that we will see on both sides of the functional and non-functional list. In this case, we are considering how we are adding functionality with the use of authentication. Later, we will see the same idea from the non-functional side to ensure we protect the assets of our application.

- **Inventory management**: The system must allow users to add, edit, and delete products.

- **Order processing**: The software should generate order confirmations and invoices.

- **Non-functional requirements**: Non-functional requirements describe how the software should perform and provide quality attributes of the system. They address aspects such as performance, scalability, security, and usability. Examples of non-functional requirements include the following:

  - **Performance**: The system should respond to user requests within three seconds

  - **Security**: Data must be encrypted both in transit and at rest

  - **Usability**: The user interface should be intuitive and accessible

- **Constraints**: Constraints are technical restrictions imposed on the software project. These constraints can be related to technical, budget, or regulatory factors. Constraints help set boundaries and guide the development process. Examples of constraints include the following:

  - **Technology stack**: The software must be developed using a specific programming language or framework

  - **Budget**: The project must not exceed a specific budget

  - **Compliance**: The software must adhere to specific industry standards or regulations

Gathering, documenting, and managing these requirements and constraints is essential throughout the software development process. They are a foundation for making design decisions, planning the project, and verifying that the final product meets the intended objectives. Practical requirement management ensures that the software meets stakeholders' expectations and business needs while addressing technical constraints and non-functional quality attributes.

Non-functional requirements and security

Non-functional requirements play a crucial role in shaping the security aspects of a software system. These requirements define how the software should perform in terms of security and specify the quality attributes related to security. Security is paramount in software development, and non-functional requirements help adequately address security considerations. Here are some examples of non-functional requirements pertaining to security and vulnerability:

- **Authentication and authorization**: Authentication requirements specify how users or entities are authenticated, such as using passwords, multi-factor authentication, or biometrics. Authorization requirements define who has access to what resources or functionalities based on roles and permissions.

- **Data security**: Encryption requirements protect sensitive data during storage, transmission, and processing. Data retention requirements specify how long data should be maintained and when and how it should be securely removed.

- **Auditability and logging**: Logging requirements dictate what events and actions must be logged for auditing purposes. Audit trail requirements ensure that logs are stored securely and are tamper-evident for later analysis.

- **Access control**: Access control requirements define how access to the system is controlled, including account lockout policies and session management.

- **Security compliance**: Compliance requirements ensure the software meets industry-specific security standards and regulations, such as GDPR, HIPAA, or ISO 27001. Each compliance organization or certification has specific non-functional requirements. An example is CI DSS, which requires the encryption of sensitive data, especially payment card information, during transmission and storage.

- **Error handling and fail-safe mechanisms**: Requirements related to error handling and fault tolerance help mitigate security risks and provide resiliency to the software by preventing system failures from exploitation.

- **Performance under attack**: The system should maintain acceptable performance even when subjected to specific security attacks, such as DDoS attacks.

- **Incident response and recovery**: Requirements should outline how the system responds to security incidents, including notification, mitigation, and recovery procedures. Later in the book, we will drill into threat modeling and think about mitigations for potential threats.

- **Scalability and load handling**: Scalability requirements ensure the system can handle increased loads without sacrificing security, preventing overload attacks.

- **Third-party integrations**: If the software interacts with third-party systems, there should be requirements for securing those integrations, including using secure APIs and data-sharing agreements.

- **Cryptography and key management**: Specify the system's cryptographic algorithms and critical management practices.

- **Physical and environmental requirements**: Specify any physical security, cooling, or power requirements.

Non-functional security requirements help shape the software's design, development, and testing, ensuring a robust and secure environment for data and users. These requirements are crucial in preventing security vulnerabilities, protecting sensitive information, and maintaining the integrity and trustworthiness of the software system.

Capturing scenarios

Software use and misuse scenarios are valuable tools in software development and security. They help identify how the software is intended to be used, abused, or misused. *Use* scenarios focus on legitimate and expected interactions with the software, while *misuse* scenarios concentrate on potential security threats and vulnerabilities. Scenarios capture specifics about the users and the systems they are interacting with. Scenarios can capture how the current systems work, or they can be visionary of how they want the system to work. Here are examples of *use* scenarios:

- **User registration**: Kate, a new user, creates an account by providing a username, email, and password, and she receives a confirmation email after the process is complete
- **Login**: A registered user, Fred, enters his account by entering his credentials into the web page
- **Product purchase**: A customer, Sally, adds items to their shopping cart, proceeds to checkout, and completes a purchase
- **Data entry**: An employee, Jim, enters data into a database, ensuring data integrity and accuracy
- **Messaging**: A user, Sarah, sends a message to another user, Marsha, and the message is delivered securely
- **File upload**: A user, Durga, uploads a file to the system, which is scanned for viruses and stored securely
- **Search**: A user, Ankish, searches for products or content, and relevant results are displayed
- **Profile update**: A user, Kisha, updates her profile information, such as her address or phone number

Here are some examples of software *misuse* scenarios:

- **Brute force attack**: An attacker, Harry, repeatedly attempts to log in with various username and password combinations to gain unauthorized access
- **SQL injection**: An attacker, Henrietta, exploits vulnerabilities in the system to inject malicious SQL queries and gain unauthorized access to the database
- **Cross-site scripting (XSS)**: An attacker, Jennifer, injects malicious scripts into user inputs, executed when other users view the page, potentially stealing their data or session information
- **Phishing**: An attacker, Seamus, sends deceptive emails or messages to trick users into revealing their login credentials or sensitive information
- **Denial of service (DoS) attack**: An attacker, Freya, overwhelms the accounting system with excessive traffic or requests, causing it to become unresponsive or unavailable to legitimate users
- **Data exfiltration**: An insider threat, Kirsten, extracts sensitive data from the system and shares it with unauthorized parties

- **Malice-in-the-middle (MitM) attack**: An attacker, Jim, intercepts communication between two parties, potentially eavesdropping or altering the transmitted data

- **Session hijacking**: An attacker, Angelina, steals a user's session cookie or token to impersonate them and gain unauthorized access to their account

- **Insider threat**: A disgruntled employee, Bob, abuses their privileges to delete or manipulate critical data or disrupt system operations

- **Third-party component vulnerabilities**: An attacker, Levi, exploits vulnerabilities in third-party libraries or components used in the software

Use and misuse scenarios guide a software system's design, testing, and security measures. They help ensure that the software can withstand common misuse and provide secure, reliable, and functional user experiences while protecting against potential threats and vulnerabilities. We will iterate back over these scenarios in our testing and validation chapters – *Chapters 11* through *13*.

Textual use cases and misuse cases

Textual use cases and misuse cases are structured descriptions of how a software system is expected to be used (use cases) and how it might be intentionally or unintentionally abused (misuse cases). They are valuable tools in software development and security analysis for understanding and documenting system behavior. Here are examples of textual use cases and misuse cases:

Textual Use Case: User registration

Title: User Registration

Primary Actor: New user

Goal: To create a new user account

Main Success Pathway:

1. The new user navigates to the registration page.

2. The new user provides a username, email, and password.

3. The system validates the provided information.

4. The system sends a confirmation email to the email address provided.

5. The new user clicks on the confirmation link in the email.

6. The system confirms the email and activates the new user account.

7. The system displays a success message.

Alternate Pathway:

If the email address is already in use, the system notifies the new user and prompts them to use a different email.

Textual Misuse Case: Brute-force attack

Title: Brute-Force Attack

Primary Actor: Attacker

Goal: To gain unauthorized access to a user's account through a brute-force attack

Main Pathway:

1. The attacker attempts to log in to a user's account by repeatedly guessing usernames and passwords.
2. The system detects multiple failed login attempts from the same IP address.

Alternate Pathway:

If the system doesn't have effective brute force detection and prevention mechanisms, the attacker may eventually succeed in guessing a valid username and password, gaining unauthorized access to the account.

Textual Use Case: Online purchase

Title: Online Purchase

Primary Actor: Customer

Goal: To complete an online purchase

Main Success Pathway:

1. The customer selects items to purchase and adds them to the shopping cart.
2. The customer proceeds to the checkout page.
3. The customer provides shipping and billing information.
4. The customer selects a payment method and enters payment details.
5. The system processes the payment and generates an order confirmation.

Alternate Pathway:

If the payment processing fails or is declined, the system provides an error message and allows the customer to retry or use an alternative payment method.

Textual Misuse Case: SQL injection

Title: SQL Injection

Primary Actor: Attacker

Goal: To exploit a SQL injection vulnerability to gain unauthorized access to the database

Main Success Pathway:

1. The attacker identifies a web form that accepts user input and doesn't correctly validate or sanitize it.
2. The attacker submits a malicious SQL query as part of the input.
3. The system processes the input without proper validation, allowing the attacker's SQL query to execute.
4. The attacker gains unauthorized access to the database and may retrieve, modify, or delete data.

Alternate Pathway:

If the system has adequate input validation and security measures, the SQL injection attempt will be blocked, and the attacker's actions will fail.

Textual use cases and misuse cases provide a structured way to document how the software should function and how it may be exploited. They serve as a basis for design, development, and security testing, helping to identify and address vulnerabilities and ensuring that the software functions as intended.

Graphical use cases and misuse cases

Graphical use and misuse cases can be represented visually in diagrams, typically using the **Unified Modeling Language** (**UML**) notations. The **Object Management Group** (**OMG**) is an international, open-membership, not-for-profit technology standards consortium. UML is one of the standards developed and maintained by the OMG.

UML use cases describe legitimate interactions with the software, while misuse cases focus on potential misuse, abuse, or security threats. Next, I'll provide examples of both graphical use cases and misuse cases.

Graphical use case diagram

In a use case diagram, you can represent use cases and actors visually. Here's a simple example:

Figure 2.1 – Example graphical use case diagram

In this diagram, the *User* actor interacts with the *Login* use case, indicating that users log in to the system.

This diagram represents a legitimate user interaction scenario.

Graphical misuse case diagram

Graphical misuse cases can also be represented in a diagram. Here's an example of a misuse case diagram:

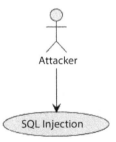

Figure 2.2 – Example misuse case diagram

In this diagram, the *Attacker* actor is associated with the *SQL Injection* misuse case, indicating that an attacker may attempt SQL injection attacks on the system.

This diagram represents a security threat scenario.

Misuse case diagrams help visualize potential security vulnerabilities or malicious actions that could compromise the system's integrity. These diagrams can be used to identify potential security risks and design countermeasures to protect against misuse cases.

Example enterprise secure functional model

Throughout this book, we will build a secure design for an event ticketing system. Envision a software system that allows a box office or a website to sell tickets to a famous musical concert or theatre event.

The following table shows a small sample of requirements for an event ticketing system.

Functional Requirements	Non-Functional Requirements	Constraints
Allow a patron to purchase tickets to an event via self-service	A patron needs to verify their email before logging in	The systems must support self-service from an iPhone device
Allow a patron to purchase multiple event tickets in the same shopping basket	The system should be able to handle 10,000 concurrent users on the website	The systems must support self-service from an Android device
Allow a box office staff member to exchange tickets between events	The system should send the confirmation email with tickets within 5 minutes of the transaction completion	Must support PayPal payments
Send an attached ticket in a confirmation email	The system should not allow self-service transactions without a verified payment	Must support PDF as a format for tickets

Table 2.1 – Sample of requirements for an event ticketing system

Next is an example use scenario for the event ticketing system.

Purchase of tickets via self-service

Sally decides to see her favorite singer perform, coming to her town in December for two nights. She visits the website for the venue on her Chromebook and picks the December 2nd performance. The system offers her three price levels (**Main Floor**, **Mezzanine**, and **Balcony**). Sally decides on the **Balcony** price level. The system shows her the available seats, and she picks **AA 101** and **AA 102**. The system shows her the total price of **$240**, where $20 is a service fee and $220 is the price for the two tickets. Sally enters her email and name as a guest user instead of logging in to an account. The system sends her a verification email since she did not log in. She pays with her Visa card. The system sends her the tickets via email with a PDF attachment.

Next, we'll see an example misuse scenario for the event ticketing system.

Trying to purchase tickets beyond the patron limit

Fred wants to purchase tickets to scalp them when a famous singer's event sells out in February. After buying the maximum tickets of 8 at the box office, he visits the website for the venue on his Android phone and picks the February 14th performance. The system offers him three price levels (**Main Floor**, **Mezzanine**, and **Balcony**). He decides on the **Main Floor** price level. The system shows him the available seats, and he picks another eight tickets. The system shows him the total price. Fred uses a different email address, enters his email as a guest user instead of logging in to an account, and uses a different credit card from the one he used at the box office. The system sends him the tickets via email with a PDF attachment.

Next is an example of a visionary use case that incorporates both of the preceding scenarios.

This is the main success pathway:

1. The patron visits the website for a venue to purchase tickets for an event.
2. The attacker submits a malicious SQL query as part of the input.
3. The system processes the input without proper validation, allowing the attacker's SQL query to execute.
4. The attacker gains unauthorized access to the database and may retrieve, modify, or delete data.

An alternate pathway is as follows:

If the system has adequate input validation and security measures, the SQL injection attempt will be blocked, and the attacker's actions will fail.

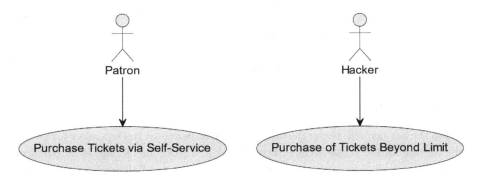

Figure 2.3 – Use case and misuse case diagram for ticketing app

We would have hundreds of scenarios, mis-scenarios, use cases, and misuse cases in an entire project. I provided enough examples to be precise but kept it simple enough so I could build on the secure, functional model in future chapters.

Summary

This chapter introduced the secure, functional model. We looked at requirement gathering, including functional, non-functional, and constraints. Next, we looked at use and misuse scenarios, which were specific textual descriptions of interactions with a system. We followed up with a more formal and generalized version of the scenarios we call textual use and misuse cases. We graphically represented these use and misuse cases with UML diagrams. Lastly, we implemented our work into an example function model for an event ticketing system.

In the next chapter, we will look at building the object model to represent the internal structure of our application.

Self-assessment questions

1. What term describes limitations or restrictions that impact the software development process?

    A. Non-functional requirements

    B. Functional requirements

    C. User stories

    D. Constraints

2. Which of the following is an example of a non-functional requirement?

    A. The system must allow users to log in with a valid username and password

    B. The system must support Internet Explorer 11

    C. The system must use the Java programming language

    D. The system must respond to user requests within 2 seconds

3. Which requirement category focuses on factors such as performance, scalability, and security?

    A. Functional requirements

    B. Non-functional requirements

    C. Business requirements

    D. User requirements

4. What type of requirement specifies the specific functions or features that a software system must perform?

    A. Non-functional requirement

    B. Technical constraint

    C. Functional requirement

    D. User interface requirement

5. Which type of requirement specifies the platforms, tools, or technologies that must be used in the software development process?

    A. Technical constraint

    B. Non-functional requirement

    C. Functional requirement

    D. Business requirement

Answers

1. D
2. D
3. B
4. C
5. A

3

Designing a Secure Object Model

Designing a secure object model is fundamental to building a secure software application. An object model represents how data and functionality are organized within your application, and ensuring its security is crucial for protecting sensitive information and preventing unauthorized access or manipulation.

In this chapter, we're going to cover security principles by looking at the following main topics:

- Identify objects and relationships
- Class diagrams
- Stereotypes
- Invariants
- Example of the enterprise secure object model

This chapter aims to empower you to decompose your software project into participating objects. In later chapters, we will build on this work to think about where the objects live and how they interact.

Identify objects and relationships

Identifying objects and decomposing your software project into participating objects from scenarios and use cases is an essential step in the analysis and design of software systems. Objects represent your system's key entities and concepts; understanding them is crucial for creating a well-structured object model. We identify objects in real life as we interact with the world, such as houses, cars, and people. Here's how you can identify objects from scenarios and use cases:

1. **Read the scenarios and use cases**: Start by carefully reading the scenarios and use cases that describe the system's functionality. These are typically written in natural language and provide a high-level overview of what the system is supposed to do.

2. **Identify nouns**: Look for nouns or noun phrases in the scenarios and use cases. These often represent potential objects in the system. For example, in a scenario describing a library, nouns such as `book`, `user`, `library`, and `catalog` could be potential objects.

3. **Pay attention to verbs**: Consider the actions or operations that must be performed in the scenarios and use cases. These actions often involve objects. For instance, if a use case mentions actions such as `borrow`, `return`, or `reserve`, they may include objects such as `book`, `user`, or `library`.

4. **Group related nouns**: Once you've identified nouns and verbs, organize related nouns involved in the same actions. For example, in a scenario about managing a bank account, you might group `Account`, `Customer`, and `Transaction` as related objects.

5. **Define object attributes**: For each identified object, think about its attributes. Attributes are the properties or characteristics of objects. For a `Customer` object, attributes might include `Name`, `Address`, and `AccountNumber`.

6. **Consider relationships**: Determine how the objects are related to each other. Relationships between objects are crucial for modeling the interactions in your system. For example, a `Book` object might be associated with a `Library` object, representing that the book is part of the library's collection.

7. **Abstract concepts**: Some objects may represent abstract concepts or system components that don't have a real-world counterpart. For example, an `OrderProcessor` object in an e-commerce system is an abstract entity responsible for processing orders.

8. **Reuse existing objects**: In many cases, you can reuse existing objects or classes if they already exist in your system libraries or frameworks. Reusing objects reduces redundancy and promotes consistency.

9. **Iterate and refine**: Identifying objects is often an iterative process. As you delve deeper into the scenarios and use cases, you may discover more objects or refine your understanding of existing ones.

10. **Document and validate**: Finally, document your identified objects, their attributes, and their relationships. Share your findings with stakeholders to ensure your object model accurately reflects the system's requirements.

Remember that this process aims to create a clear and comprehensive object model that accurately represents the system's functionality and structure. Maintaining consistency and alignment with your software project's requirements and design principles is essential. We can start by just listing objects in our domain. For example, a library system has patrons, books, librarians, and so on. We will next look at a predominant object modeling notation that will allow us to think about our objects and iterate over our model, adding more semantics as we drill down.

Class diagrams

Class diagrams are a fundamental part of the **Unified Modeling Language** (**UML**) and depict the structure and relationships of the classes within a system or software application. UML is a modeling language maintained by the **Object Management Group** (**OMG**). Class diagrams are a valuable tool for visualizing, designing, and documenting the architecture of your software. In this context, a class is like a blueprint for the objects we will use in our software. The class is the blueprint, and the object is the instance of that blueprint. Here are some key elements and concepts in class diagrams:

- **Class**: The central element in a class diagram is the class itself, represented as a rectangle with three compartments, as shown in *Figure 3.1*:

    - The top compartment contains the class's name

    - The middle compartment lists the class's attributes or properties

    - The bottom compartment displays the class's methods or operations

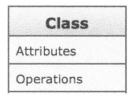

Figure 3.1 – UML class notation

- **Attributes**: Attributes are the data members or properties of a class. They are typically listed in the middle compartment of the class box and include the attribute name and data type. For example, an `Employee` class may have attributes such as `ID` (integer) and `Name` (string). Attributes are shown in the second section, as shown in *Figure 3.1*.

- **Methods**: Methods are the operations or functions that a class can perform. They are listed in the bottom compartment of the class box, including the method name, input parameters, and return type. For instance, an `Order` class may have methods such as `calculateTotal()` and `placeOrder(item: Item): boolean`. Operations or methods are shown in the third section, as shown in *Figure 3.1*.

- **Associations**: Associations represent the relationships between classes. They are shown as lines connecting classes with optional arrows to indicate the direction of the association. Multiplicity notations (e.g., `1`, `*`, `0..1`) can be added to specify how many objects of one class are related to objects of another class. For example, an association between `Customer` and `Order` classes may indicate that customers can have multiple orders. *Figure 3.2* shows the different association relationships represented in UML class diagrams.

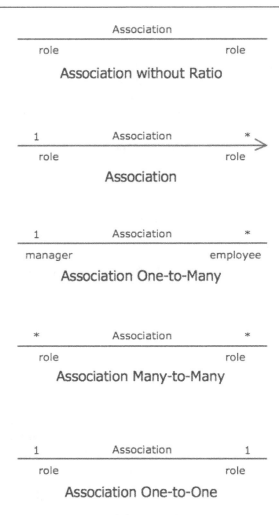

Figure 3.2 – UML association notation

- **Aggregation**: Aggregation is a type of association that represents a whole-part relationship. It is shown as a diamond shape on the class containing the whole, connected to the class containing the part. For instance, in a class diagram for the Car and Wheel classes, you might use aggregation to show that a car has wheels. *Figure 3.3* shows an example of the UML aggregation notation.

Figure 3.3 – UML aggregation notation

- **Composition**: Composition is a more vital form of aggregation that signifies a strong ownership relationship. A diamond shape also represents it, but the diamond is filled with a solid color. It implies that the whole (composite) class controls the creation and destruction of its part (component) class—for example, a House class composed of Room classes. *Figure 3.4* shows an example of the UML composition notation.

Figure 3.4 – UML composition notation

- **Inheritance** (generalization): Inheritance represents an *is-a* relationship between classes. It is displayed as an arrow with a hollow triangle pointing from the subclass to the superclass. The superclass is often referred to as the **base class** or **parent class**, and the subclass is the **derived class** or **child class**. *Figure 3.5* shows an example of the UML inheritance notation.

Figure 3.5 – UML inheritance notation

- **Interfaces**: Interfaces define a contract of methods a class must implement. In class diagrams, interfaces are represented as a lollipop shape, and a dashed line connects the interface to the implementing classes. *Figure 3.6* shows the notation for a UML interface.

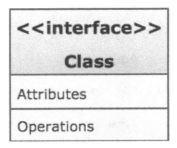

Figure 3.6 – UML interface notation

- **Dependencies**: Dependencies indicate a relationship where one class relies on another but not through inheritance, aggregation, or association. Dependencies are represented as dashed arrows pointing from the dependent class to the class it depends on. *Figure 3.7* shows an example of the UML dependency notation.

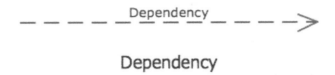

Dependency

Figure 3.7 – UML dependency notation

- **Packages**: Class diagrams can be organized into packages for grouping related classes. Folders or rectangles typically represent packages, which help manage the complexity of large systems. *Figure 3.8* shows an example of the UML package notation.

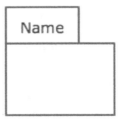

Figure 3.8 – UML package notation

Here is a simple example of a UML class diagram for a library management system to give you an idea of what it might look like.

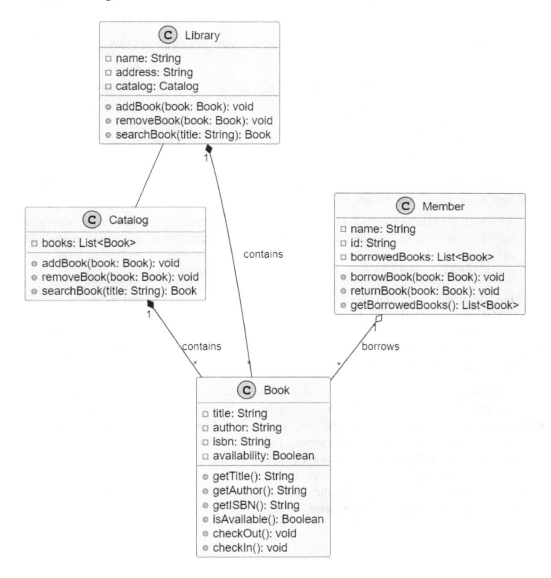

Figure 3.9 – Example UML class diagram for a library system

In this diagram, we have the following:

- The `Library` class represents the library and has attributes such as `name`, `address`, and `catalog`.

- The `Catalog` class represents the catalog of books in the library and contains a list of books.

- The `Book` class represents a book with attributes such as `title`, `author`, `ISBN`, and `availability`. It also has methods for checking in and checking out a book.

- The `Member` class represents a library member who can borrow and return books. Each class is depicted as a rectangle with three compartments: the top compartment contains the class name, the middle compartment lists the class attributes, and the bottom compartment lists the class methods or operations.

- Arrows (lines) connect the classes to indicate relationships. For example, `Book` and `Member` have associations with the library management system.

- After each attribute or method is a data type. For the attributes, this is the data type that can be stored in the attribute. For the method, this is the type of data returned from the method. In the example UML class diagram, `String` represents alphanumeric data, `Boolean` is either `true` or `false`, and `Void` means a method does not return a value.

The library object model is a simple example. In a real-world library management system, you would likely have more classes, attributes, methods, associations, and multiplicity indicators to specify the relationships between classes more precisely. UML diagrams can be created using various UML modeling tools, such as Lucidchart and draw.io, or dedicated UML software such as Sparx Systems Enterprise Architect or IBM Rational Software Architect.

Class diagrams are a versatile tool for designing and documenting the structure of your software system, making them a valuable part of the UML notation. They visually represent classes and their attributes, methods, and relationships, helping software developers and architects communicate and design software more effectively. The process presented in this book is iterative. We will revisit the UML class diagram in *Chapter 3*, where we discuss the dynamic model of the operations classes needed to support it. *Chapter 3* will also discuss tooling that can be used to develop the class diagram we discussed in this chapter, along with other UML diagram types. In *Chapter 4*, we package classes together into partitions and discuss the system model.

Stereotypes

UML allows you to extend and customize its standard notations and semantics through stereotypes. Stereotypes are a way to add domain-specific or application-specific information to your UML models. When representing security requirements in UML, you can use stereotypes to indicate specific security-related elements or aspects within your diagrams. Developers use common stereotypes, but it is essential to realize you can build your own and are not limited to the common ones. Here are some common UML stereotypes and how they can be used to represent security requirements:

- `<<security>>`: This stereotype can be applied to various UML elements to indicate that they have security implications. Here are some examples:

    - A class with `<<security>>` stereotype might imply that it contains sensitive data or requires access control

    - A use case with `<<security>>` stereotype may indicate that it involves authentication or authorization

- `<<secure>>`: Use this stereotype to mark classes, components, or other critical elements in the system's security. Here are some examples:

    - A component with `<<secure>>` stereotype could represent a security module or subsystem

    - A class with `<<secure>>` stereotype might indicate it's involved in cryptographic operations

- `<<sensitive>>`: Apply this stereotype to attributes or properties of a class to denote that they hold sensitive information or data that requires protection. For instance, a class called `User` with a `SocialSecurityNumber` attribute tagged as `<<sensitive>>` indicates that this attribute is sensitive and must be protected.

- `<<security-constraint>>`: Use this stereotype to represent security constraints or policies within the system. These constraints may include access control rules, data encryption policies, and authentication requirements.

- `<<threat>>`: Stereotype instances of this type can be used to represent security threats, such as SQL injection, **cross-site scripting** (**XSS**), or brute-force attacks. These can be associated with use cases or components to document potential threats.

- `<<mitigation>>`: Stereotype this to indicate how specific threats or vulnerabilities are mitigated within the system. You can use it to describe the security measures to address threats or vulnerabilities.

- `<<security-control>>`: This stereotype can represent specific security controls, such as firewalls, intrusion detection systems, or authentication mechanisms. Apply it to components or classes that provide security mechanisms.

- `<<authorization>>` and `<<authentication>>`: These stereotypes can be used to mark use cases or components involved in user authentication or authorization processes.

- `<<crypto>>`: Use this stereotype to specify that a particular class or component is related to cryptographic operations and requires security consideration.

- `<<audit>>`: Stereotype components or use cases related to audit trails, monitoring, or logging for security and compliance purposes.

In addition to using stereotypes, you can also use tagged values to provide more specific information related to security requirements within your UML models. For example, you can use tagged values to specify the encryption algorithm or authentication mechanism employed. We will revisit this in the dynamic model and system model chapters (3 and 4).

By incorporating these UML stereotypes and tagged values, you can effectively model and document security requirements, vulnerabilities, and countermeasures in your software design, making it easier to communicate and ensure that security concerns are addressed during the development process.

Invariants

Object Constraint Language (OCL) is a textual language used for specifying constraints, conditions, and expressions on UML models. OCL invariants are rules and constraints that define conditions that must be true for objects and their relationships within a UML model. Invariants play a crucial role in ensuring the correctness and integrity of a UML model. Here are some critical points about OCL invariants:

- **Syntax**: OCL invariants are typically expressed using a well-defined syntax. They follow a format similar to predicate logic and often use keywords such as `inv` (for invariant) to specify that a condition must hold.

- **Usage**: Invariants can be applied to various elements of a UML model, including classes, associations, attributes, and operations. They provide a way to specify constraints that must be satisfied by instances of these elements.

- **Invariant examples**:

  - Class invariants: You can specify invariants on a UML class to define conditions that should always be true for instances of that class:

    ```
    context BankAccount
    inv: balance >= 0
    ```

- Attribute invariants: Invariants can be used to define constraints on class attributes. For instance, you can ensure that an attribute always has a specific format:

```
context PhoneNumber
inv: self.matches(/^\d{3}-\d{3}-\d{4}$/)
```

- Association invariants: You can define invariants for UML associations to specify constraints on object relationships. For example, you can enforce that a bidirectional relationship exists:

```
context BidirectionalRelationship
inv: self.opposite.opposite = self
```

- **Context**: The `context` keyword is used to specify the element to which the invariant applies. It defines the context in which the invariant is evaluated.

- **Self**: The `self` keyword refers to the object the invariant applies to. It allows you to access the properties and relationships of the current object.

- **Logical Expressions**: OCL supports various logical and comparison operators (e.g., `and`, `or`, `not`, `=`, `<`, `>`) that can build complex conditions within invariants.

- **Constraints Checking**: In practice, tools and UML modeling environments often support the automatic validation of OCL invariants. The UML model is automatically checked against the defined invariants to ensure compliance. Violations can be flagged as errors or warnings.

- **Documentation**: Invariants should be well documented to explain their purpose and the conditions they enforce. Documentation is essential for making the UML model understandable and maintainable.

OCL invariants are a powerful tool for specifying and enforcing constraints within UML models. They help ensure the integrity and consistency of your models, making them a valuable aspect of UML modeling in software engineering.

Example of the enterprise secure object model

Throughout this book, we will build a secure design for an event ticketing system. Envision a software system that allows a box office or a website to sell tickets to a famous musical concert or theatre event.

The following figure shows a small sample of classes, relationships, and attributes for our ongoing event ticketing system example.

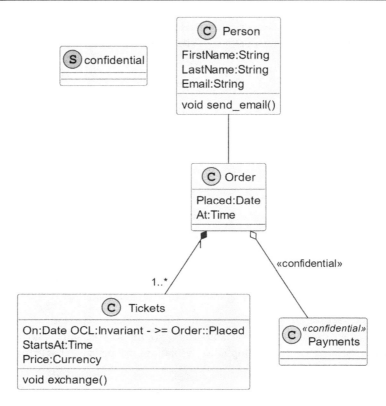

Figure 3.10 – Example UML class diagram

This example has four classes represented by the boxes with Cs. The guillemets (double chevrons, << >>) and the word confidential represent one stereotype. In this example, the stereotype is applied to the aggregation of payments by the Order class and directly to the Payments class. The lines show an association between customers and orders. The diamonds at the end of the lines between order, tickets, and payment classes show the aggregation. Aggregations are generally represented as one-to-many in the code. The On attribute in the tickets class has an OCL invariant that says the ticket date is always greater than or equal to the Placed attribute on the Order class. The invariant represents a requirement you must purchase for future events, not events that have already occurred.

The example also has a few methods or operations. For example, we can email a patron with the send_email method or exchange tickets with the exchange method. In our dynamic model discussion in *Chapter 4*, we will revisit many more methods but in the object model phase, we designate the methods we already know exist.

Again, this is a small portion of classes that would be involved in the object model for a complete system for event ticketing.

Summary

This chapter introduced the secure object model. We looked at modeling classes, attributes, and relationships in UML class diagrams. Next, we looked at adding stereotypes to have more meaning represented in the diagram. We followed up with the addition of OCL invariants.

In the next chapter, we will build a dynamic model for message passing in our application.

Self-assessment questions

1. What is the primary purpose of a UML class diagram?

    A. To describe the deployment of software components on hardware

    B. To display the flow of control within a software application

    C. To show the sequence of interactions between objects

    D. D. To represent the structure and relationships of classes in a system

2. In a UML class diagram, what does a solid line with an arrowhead between two classes represent?

    A. Composition

    B. Inheritance (generalization)

    C. Association

    D. Aggregation

3. Which UML class diagram relationship implies strong ownership, where the child class cannot exist without the parent class?

    A. Aggregation

    B. Generalization

    C. Association

    D. Composition

4. What is the purpose of multiplicity notation in a UML class diagram?

    A. To represent the nesting level of classes within a package

    B. To indicate the number of methods in a class

    C. To specify the visibility of attributes and methods

    D. To show how many instances of one class can be associated with another

5.   Which UML class diagram element is used to represent a behavior or function that an object can perform?

A.   Association

B.   Attribute

C.   Dependency

D.   Method

6.   In UML, what is the purpose of a stereotype when applied to a class or an interface?

A.   To specify the number of instances of the class

B.   To indicate the class's visibility

C.   To define the relationships between classes

D.   To extend or modify the semantics of the class or interface

7.   Which of the following is an example of a stereotype commonly used in UML to represent a user-defined constraint or tagged value?

A.   «implements»

B.   «association»

C.   «constraint»

D.   «extends»

8.   What is the primary purpose of OCL in software engineering and modeling?

A.   To specify constraints and invariants on UML models

B.   To create object-oriented programming code from UML diagrams

C.   To represent the flow of control in a software system

D.   To define classes and their relationships in a UML diagram

9.   In OCL, what does the `pre` keyword signify when used in a constraint expression?

A.   It represents the post-condition of an operation

B.   It is used to denote an invariant.

C.   It refers to a precondition that must be held before an operation is executed

D.   It indicates a constraint that applies after an operation has been executed

10. Which of the following is a valid OCL expression for specifying that the age attribute of a Person class should always be greater than or equal to 18?

    A. age.Person >= 18

    B. Person.age => 18

    C. Person.age >= 18

    D. 18 <= Person.age

Answers

1. D
2. C
3. D
4. D
5. D
6. D
7. C
8. A
9. C
10. C

4

Designing a Secure Dynamic Model

Designing a secure dynamic model is critical for building a secure software application or IT infrastructure. The dynamic model defines interactions between the objects in the system.

In this chapter, we're going to cover designing a secure dynamic model by looking at the following main topics:

- Object behavior
- Modeling interactions between objects
- Constraints
- Example of the enterprise secure dynamic model

The goal of this chapter is to discover objects we may have missed in the object design, along with exploring the methods the objects need to support by thinking about how objects interact.

Technical requirements

Unified Modeling Language (UML) tools are software applications designed to facilitate the creation and manipulation of UML diagrams. UML is a standardized modeling language used in software engineering for visualizing, specifying, constructing, and documenting the artifacts of a software system.

Here are some popular UML tools:

- Enterprise Architect is a comprehensive UML modeling tool that supports various diagram types and is widely used for software development, business process modeling, and system engineering.
- Visual Paradigm provides a suite of tools for software development, including UML modeling, business process modeling, and system architecture design.

- IBM Rational Software Architect is part of the IBM Rational software development platform. It supports UML modeling and is used for architectural design, modeling, and development of software applications.

- Astah is a lightweight and user-friendly UML modeling tool that supports a variety of UML diagrams. It is suitable for both beginners and experienced modelers.

- Lucidchart is a web-based diagramming tool that supports UML diagrams, flowcharts, and other visualizations. It is easy to use and collaborative.

- Draw.io is an open source web-based diagramming tool that supports UML diagrams and various other diagram types. It can be used directly in a web browser.

- StarUML is an open source UML tool that supports the UML 2.x standard. It provides a user-friendly interface and allows the creation of various UML diagrams.

- PlantUML is a text-based UML diagramming tool that defines diagrams using a simple and human-readable language. It supports various diagram types, and the diagrams can be generated from textual descriptions.

When choosing a UML tool, consider the specific UML diagrams you need, collaboration features, ease of use, integration with other development tools, and cost. Additionally, the choice may depend on personal preference and the specific requirements of your project or organization.

Object behavior

Designing object behavior is a critical aspect of object-oriented software development. Object behavior refers to how objects of a class interact with one another and the system as a whole. In our object identification in the previous chapter, we listed some operations, but we want to dig in and discover how our objects interact. Here are some considerations for designing object behavior:

- Identify objects and classes:

  - You can begin by identifying the objects and classes in your system. These represent the entities and concepts that your software will model. We focused on this in *Chapter 3*. One example from our event ticketing system is the Person object, which represents the patrons' purchasing tickets. We also have previously identified Orders, Tickets, and Payment classes. *Figure 4.17* later in this chapter shows an updated version of the UML class diagram from *Chapter 3*.

- Define object responsibilities:

  - Determine what each object's responsibilities are. What tasks or actions should each object be able to perform? For example, an account would need to allow for deposits and withdrawals in a banking example. A second example would be a ticket going from available to sold with a purchase in our ticketing example.

- Consider the behavior an object should exhibit when specific methods are called. What should happen when you invoke a method on an object? State diagrams are terrific models for observing the state change based on method invocation. To explore this idea, consider our Ticket object identified in the previous chapter. When a ticket is purchased, the seat will no longer be available for others to buy. *Figure 4.1* shows a state diagram where a purchase and return move between states of the ticket.

Ticketing System - State of a Ticket

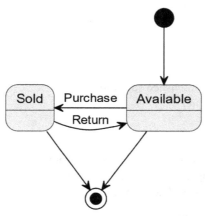

Figure 4.1 – State diagram for a ticket

- Specify object interfaces:

  - Define the public interface of each object. What methods and properties should be exposed to other objects? Examples include public and private visibility and the specific data types sent to the method.

  - Think about the inputs and outputs of each method. What parameters should methods accept, and what should they return? In our example, an example is the `add_tickets` method of the `Order` class that takes in an input of quantity expressed as an integer. You may have listed methods in earlier phases, but in the dynamic modeling, we want to iterate and draw out these details.

- Use UML diagrams:

  - Utilize UML diagrams, such as sequence or state diagrams, to visualize and document objects' behavior and interactions. Throughout this book, we are utilizing UML to provide the models.

  - Sequence diagrams can be beneficial in showing the chronological order of method calls between objects. Later in this chapter, we will drill into sequence diagrams.

- Encapsulation:

  - Encapsulation adds a layer of abstraction so changes in the object do not require changes in the user.

  - Enforce encapsulation to hide the internal details of an object's behavior and protect its state. Often, encapsulation is done by setting attributes to private and providing methods to get and set the values.

  - Determine which attributes should be private and accessible via getters and setters. Visibility of attributes and methods.

- Design patterns:

  - Consider using design patterns to solve common problems related to object behavior. Patterns provide well-established solutions to recurring design challenges. We will explore design patterns in *Chapter 5*.

- Collaboration:

  - Identify how objects collaborate and communicate with each other to accomplish system tasks. Later in this chapter, we will drill into sequence diagrams. Sequence diagrams allow you to model the messages that are passed between objects to accomplish the process.

  - Define the rules and protocols for interaction, including message passing, method calls, and event handling.

- State and state transitions:

  - If objects have different states, define the states and transitions between them

  - Use state diagrams to visualize the possible states and the conditions for transitioning between them

- Error handling:

  - Consider how objects should handle errors and exceptions. Define the behavior for error conditions and how objects should recover or propagate errors to higher levels.

- Testing and validation:

  - Develop test cases that validate the behavior of objects and their interactions. We will revisit this in the third part of the book, when we look at validating the requirements and models we are specifying in this section.

  - Unit, integration, and system tests can help ensure that objects behave as expected.

- Documentation:

  - Document the expected behavior of objects. This documentation should include method descriptions, preconditions, postconditions, and any invariants that must be maintained.

- Refinement and iteration:

  - Designing object behavior is often an iterative process. As the design evolves, revisit and refine the behavior of objects as needed.

- Pattern recognition:

  - Over time, you may develop a sense of recognizing common patterns of object behavior in your domain. Reusing successful patterns can improve design efficiency and quality.

In summary, designing object behavior involves identifying objects, specifying their responsibilities, defining their interfaces, and ensuring they collaborate effectively to fulfill system requirements. It's a crucial aspect of object-oriented design, and careful consideration and planning are essential for creating a well-structured and maintainable software system.

Modeling interactions between objects

Modeling interactions between objects is a fundamental aspect of object-oriented software design. It involves defining how objects communicate, collaborate, and work together to achieve the functionality of a software system. To model interactions effectively, you can use various techniques and diagrams. What follows are modeling techniques you can use to model object interactions. We explored use case diagrams in *Chapter 2*; we will explore several other models in this chapter and the next.

- Use case diagrams: Use case diagrams to assist you in modeling the interactions between the system and its actors. Actors can be users or external systems that interact with the software. Use cases represent specific interactions between the actors and the system, showing what functionality is available and how it's accessed. In *Chapter 2*, we talked a lot about textual use cases and graphical use cases.

- Sequence diagrams: Sequence diagrams are a powerful tool for modeling the dynamic behavior of a system by showing how objects interact over time. They depict the sequence of messages and method calls between objects, illustrating the control and data flow.

- Collaboration diagrams (communication diagrams): Collaboration diagrams are similar to sequence diagrams but focus on the relationships and interactions between objects rather than the chronological order of messages. They emphasize object structure and show how objects are connected.

- Activity diagrams: Activity diagrams are helpful for modeling interactions that involve complex activities or processes. They allow you to represent workflows, decisions, and parallel flows in an interaction. Activity diagrams are often used to model business processes. We will drill into activity diagrams later in this chapter.

- State diagrams: State diagrams help model objects' state transitions and behavior. They are useful when objects exhibit different behaviors or states during interactions. State diagrams show how objects change states in response to events or actions.

- Use collaboration and sequence diagrams: Collaboration diagrams represent objects' static structure and associations, while sequence diagrams illustrate how these objects interact in a dynamic context. Combining them can provide a comprehensive view of interactions.

- Communication patterns: Identify common communication patterns between objects, such as client-server interactions, observer patterns, publisher-subscriber patterns, and request-response patterns. Recognizing these patterns can simplify interaction modeling.

- Responsibilities and interfaces: Clearly define the responsibilities of each object and the interfaces they expose for communication. The definition is essential for specifying how objects interact with each other.

- Message passing: Describe the messages and method calls exchanged between objects. Include details about the message content, parameters, and the expected behavior of the receiving object.

- Error handling: Model how objects handle errors and exceptions during interactions. Define the behavior of objects when things go wrong and how they communicate error information to other objects or systems.

- Interaction scenarios: Create interaction scenarios to document specific sequences of interactions, covering various use cases and exceptional conditions. Scenarios help ensure that the system behaves as intended.

- Testing and validation: Use the interaction models to create test cases and validate that the interactions between objects are working correctly. Unit, integration, and system testing are essential for verifying the system's behavior.

- Documentation: Ensure that interaction models and diagrams are well-documented. This documentation should include descriptions of interactions, roles, and responsibilities of objects, and any constraints or rules governing interactions.

Modeling interactions between objects is crucial for understanding the behavior and flow of a software system. Effective interaction modeling can improve software design, system implementation, and maintainability.

Next, we will look at a few of the interactivity models I use the most in my secure software development work.

UML sequence diagrams

A UML sequence diagram is a type of interaction diagram that visualizes the interactions and message exchanges between various objects and components within a system over a specific period. Sequence diagrams are commonly used to illustrate the dynamic behavior of a system, showing how objects collaborate to accomplish tasks or scenarios. Here is an overview of the critical elements and conventions of a UML sequence diagram:

- Objects (lifelines): Objects or lifelines represent the entities, components, or instances involved in the interaction. Each object is depicted as a vertical line (lifeline) with its name or identifier at the top, extending vertically to show its existence over time. Time starts at the top and moves down. *Figure 4.2* shows an object with a lifeline.

Figure 4.2 – UML lifeline

- Activation bar: An activation bar is a horizontal bar that extends from the lifeline to represent the period during which an object is actively involved in processing or responding to messages. *Figure 4.3* shows a UML activation bar.

Figure 4.3 – UML activation bar

- Messages: Messages are arrows and lines that depict communication and interactions between objects. Messages can be synchronous (blocking) or asynchronous (non-blocking). *Figure 4.4* shows examples of the message notation.

  Synchronous messages are represented by solid arrows with a filled arrowhead and indicate that the sender waits for the receiver to process the message. Asynchronous messages are depicted with a dashed line and an open arrowhead, showing that the sender does not wait for a response from the receiver.

Figure 4.4 – UML messages

- Return messages: Return messages indicate the response from the receiver to a previously received message. They are often depicted as dashed lines returning to the original sender. *Figure 4.5* shows a return message.

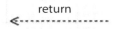

Figure 4.5 – UML return message

- Self-call (recursive call): A self-call is a message sent from an object to itself, representing an internal action or recursive function call. A loopback arrow indicates the self-call. A recursive self-call is represented with an extra activation bar.

  Figure 4.6 shows both types of self-messages.

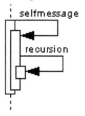

Figure 4.6 – UML self message

- Creation message: A creation message shows the creation of a new object or instance within the diagram. It is typically represented by a solid arrow with a bar (X) at the receiving end. *Figure 4.7* shows a UML create message.

Figure 4.7 – UML create message

- Destroy message: A destroy message signifies the termination or destruction of an object. It is shown by an X at the sender's end of the lifeline.

- Notes and comments: Sequence diagrams can include notes and comments to provide additional information and explanations about the interactions and messages.

- Interaction fragments (optional): Interaction fragments, such as combined fragments (e.g., alt, opt, loop) and interaction operands, can represent conditional or repetitive behavior within the sequence diagram.

Here's a simple example of a UML sequence diagram:

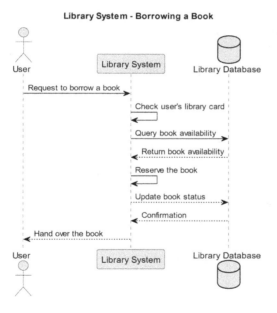

Figure 4.8 – Example of a sequence diagram

In this diagram, we have the following:

- Lifelines represent three objects, User, Library System, and Library Database

- Messages are exchanged between these objects to illustrate the interactions

- An activation bar shows the period when an object actively processes messages
- The return message indicates the response to a previously sent message

Let's go through this scenario:

1. The user requests to borrow a book from the library system.
2. The library system checks the user's library card.
3. The library system queries the library database for book availability.
4. The library database responds with book availability information.
5. The library system reserves the book.
6. The library system updates the book status in the database.
7. The library database confirms the reservation.
8. Finally, the library system hands over the book to the user.

Sequence diagrams are invaluable for capturing and visualizing the dynamic aspects of a system, such as the order of method calls and message flows, making them a valuable tool for system design, analysis, and documentation.

Next, let's look at activity diagrams, which will allow us to model the program flow along with the data flow.

UML activity diagrams

A UML activity diagram is a graphical representation used to model and visualize the flow of activities or actions within a system or a business process. Activity diagrams are versatile and can be used for various purposes, including modeling workflow, business processes, and system behavior. Here are the key elements and conventions of UML activity diagrams:

Initial Node

Figure 4.9 – UML initial node

Initial node: The diagram typically starts with an initial node, represented by a solid circle, indicating the activity's beginning. *Figure 4.9* shows an initial node.

- Action or activity: Activities represent actions or steps in the process. They are depicted as rounded rectangles with the action's name inside. Actions can be simple, such as calculations, or complex, involving sub-activities. *Figure 4.10* shows a UML action or activity node.

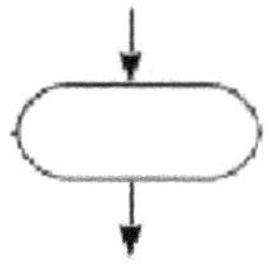

Action Node

Figure 4.10 – UML action node

- Decision and merge nodes: Decision nodes, represented as diamonds, are used to model conditional behavior. Merge nodes are used to show where different branches of the decision converge. *Figure 4.11* shows a merge node. If more than one arrow leaves the diamond it is a decision node.

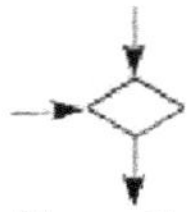

Merge Node

Figure 11 – UML merge node

- Fork and join nodes: Fork nodes (horizontal bars) represent the simultaneous start of multiple activities, while join nodes (horizontal bars with a small notch) show where concurrent activities synchronize. *Figure 4.12* shows a UML fork node. Like the earlier distinction for decision and merge nodes, if multiple arrows are entering the bar then it is a join node.

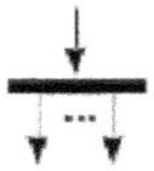

Fork Node

Figure 4.12 – UML fork node

- Flow arrows: Arrows connecting elements represent the control flow between activities. Arrows typically indicate the order in which actions are executed or the conditions under which flows occur.

- Control flow: A solid arrow represents the default control flow from one activity to another. Dashed arrows are used to show alternative flows or exceptions.

- Decision and merge edges: Decision edges (coming out of decision nodes) are labeled with a guard condition in square brackets, indicating the condition for taking a particular branch. Merge edges (coming into merge nodes) show where the flows converge.

- Final node: A final node, represented as a circle with a dot inside, denotes the end of the activity or process. *Figure 4.13* shows a UML final node.

Final Node

Figure 4.13 – UML final node

- Object nodes: Object nodes can represent objects or data used in the activities. They are often shown as rectangles with the name of the object or data type.

- Partition (swimlane): Partitions, or swimlanes, can group activities performed by different roles, systems, or entities. They are represented as vertical or horizontal bands.

- Parallel processing: Dotted lines can indicate parallel processing of activities that coincide. This notation is handy for showing concurrency in workflows.

- Expansion region: Expansion regions represent loops, iterations, and parallel executions of activities.

Figure 4.14 shows a simplified example of a UML activity diagram for a library system. The model is a simple flow of a user attempting to check out a book from the library.

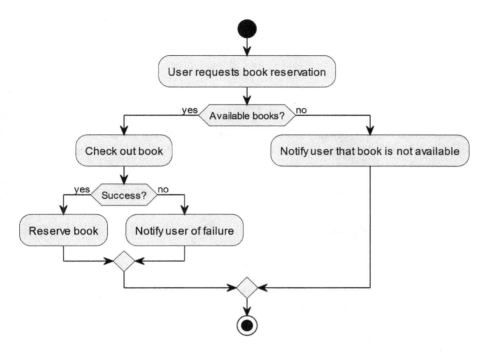

Figure 4.14 – An activity diagram

In this diagram, we have the following:

- The initial node indicates the start of the process
- Activities such as "User requests book reservation" and "Notify user book is not available" represent actions within the system
- The decision node "Success?" determines the flow based on a condition
- The final node marks the end of the process

UML activity diagrams are valuable tools for modeling processes, workflows, and a system's or business process's dynamic behavior. The activity diagrams help understand, document, and communicate complex processes and can be used during system design, analysis, and development phases.

Constraints

In the context of UML, **Object Constraint Language** (**OCL**) is often used to define preconditions and postconditions for operations (methods) of a class. Preconditions and postconditions specify the requirements that must be satisfied before and after an operation is invoked. They help ensure the operation's behavior is well-defined and adheres to certain constraints. Here's an explanation of preconditions and postconditions in OCL:

- Preconditions:

  - Preconditions define conditions that must be true before an operation can be executed. They describe the state of the system or object that must be in place for the operation to proceed.

  - Preconditions are typically specified using OCL expressions and are associated with a specific operation in a UML class diagram. These expressions are evaluated before the operation is executed.

  - If a precondition is not satisfied when the operation is invoked, the system should prevent the operation from executing and report an error.

  Here's an example of preconditions in OCL:

  ```
  OCL context BankAccount::withdraw(amount: Real)
  pre: amount > 0 and balance >= amount
  ```

  In this example, the precondition specifies that the withdraw operation on a BankAccount object can only be executed if the withdrawal amount is greater than zero. In other words, the account balance is sufficient to cover the withdrawal. It also ensures there is a balance equal to or greater than the amount being withdrawn.

- Postconditions:

  - Postconditions describe the state of the system or object after the operation has been executed. They specify the expected outcomes, results, or invariants that should be true after the operation is completed.

  - Postconditions are also expressed using OCL and are associated with a specific operation. These expressions are evaluated after the operation has been executed.

  - Postconditions validate that the operation produced the desired effect and that the system is in a valid state after the operation.

  Here is an example of postconditions in OCL:

  ```
  OCL context BankAccount::deposit(amount: Real)
  post: balance = self.balance@pre + amount
  ```

  In this example, the postcondition states that after the deposit operation on a BankAccount, the new balance should equal the previous balance plus the deposited amount.

Preconditions and postconditions play a vital role in ensuring the correctness and reliability of software systems. They provide a formal way to document and validate the expected behavior of operations. During testing and verification, preconditions and postconditions can be used to check whether the operation behaves as specified. Violations of preconditions or postconditions can help identify defects or errors in the system.

Example of the enterprise secure dynamic model

Throughout this book, we will build a secure design for an event ticketing system. Envision a software system that allows a box office or a website to sell tickets to a famous musical concert or theatre event.

Figure 4.15 shows an example sequence diagram for a simple ticket purchase:

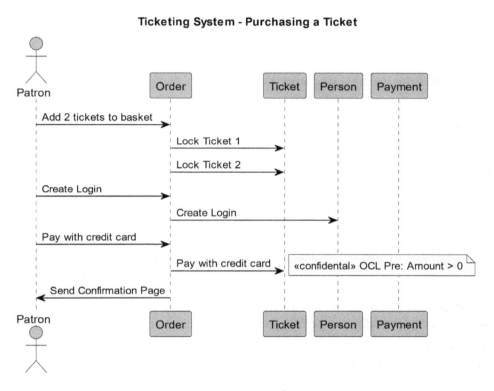

Figure 4.15 – Sequence diagram for ticket purchase

In the diagram, the patron requests to add tickets to the order. The Order class passes the request on to the ticket class for each ticket to lock the ticket so others cannot purchase. After the tickets are locked, the patron requests to create a login. The login is passed onto the Person class. Next, the patron pays with a credit card. The message is passed from the Order class to the Payment class, and we see the stereotype and OCL pre-condition marked in the note. At the end, a confirmation page is passed back to the patron.

Figure 4.16 shows an activity diagram for purchasing a ticket with the event ticketing system.

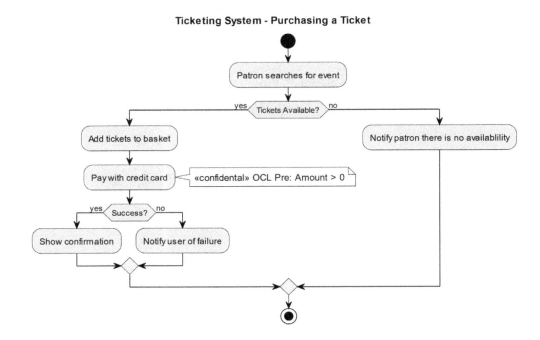

Figure 4.16 – Purchasing a Ticket activity diagram

The flow starts with a search for events. If there is no availability, the activity will end. Otherwise, the tickets are added to the basket. This activity is followed by an attempt to pay. In the payment, we see both the stereotype for confidentiality and the OCL precondition to ensure the amount is greater than zero.

After the dynamic model exposed the classes' interactivity, we updated previous models with the discovered operations. *Figure 4.17* shows an updated class diagram for the event ticketing system example project. We added new classes and methods to classes we discovered in our dynamic modeling phase. For example, we discovered that the Person class needed the create_login method, the Order class needed the add_payment and add_tickets methods, and so on.

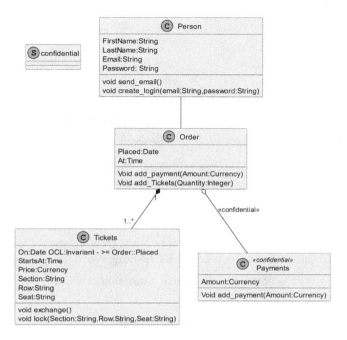

Figure 4.17 – Updated ticketing class diagram

The updated class diagram is probably just a small subset of all the classes that would be in a true enterprise ticketing system. What we wanted to show here is the iterative additions of additional methods.

Summary

This chapter introduces the secure, dynamic model. The dynamic model aims to discover the interactions between classes and missing classes in our previous models. We discussed many different models that can be used for the dynamic model, but we drilled into examples with sequence and activity diagrams. We utilized the information we discovered in this modeling to update previous models with this new information. In the next chapter, we will look at the system model and how we should partition our systems. We will also build the object model to represent the internal structure of our application.

Self-assessment questions

1. In a UML sequence diagram, what does a lifeline represent, and how is it typically depicted?

    A. A lifeline represents a message exchange between two objects and is depicted as a solid horizontal line.

    B. A lifeline represents the lifespan of an object and is depicted as a dashed vertical line.

C. A lifeline represents the sequence of actions within an operation and is depicted as a dashed horizontal line.

D. A lifeline represents the class diagram and is depicted as a solid vertical line.

2. What is the purpose of an activation bar in a UML sequence diagram?

A. To represent the inheritance relationship between classes in the system

B. To display the message parameters passed between objects

C. To highlight the interactions between different use cases

D. To indicate the duration of a message's execution by showing a horizontal bar above the lifeline

3. In a UML sequence diagram, what does a return message indicate, and how is it represented?

A. A return message indicates a synchronous response from the receiver object to the sender object and is represented by a dashed arrow pointing back to the sender's lifeline.

B. A return message indicates the creation of a new object and is represented by a dashed horizontal line.

C. A return message is used to represent the inclusion of a use case and is represented by a solid arrow pointing to the included use case.

D. A return message indicates the termination of an object's lifeline and is represented by a solid horizontal line.

4. What is the primary purpose of an activity diagram in UML?

A. To model the interaction between different objects in a system

B. To show the static structure of a system's classes and their relationships

C. To visualize the flow of activities and actions in a system or process

D. To represent the timing and synchronization of concurrent processes

5. In an activity diagram, what does a diamond-shaped symbol represent, and how is it typically used?

A. An initial node indicates the starting point of the diagram and is where control flow begins.

B. A final node marks the end of the entire diagram, indicating the completion of the activity.

C. A fork node signifies the beginning of concurrent activities that can be executed in parallel.

D. A decision node represents a point in the diagram where a choice is made between multiple alternative paths.

6. What is the purpose of an activity partition in an activity diagram, and how is it represented?

    A. An activity partition is used to define a sequence of actions, and it is represented as a rectangle with rounded corners.

    B. An activity partition is a placeholder for external interactions with other systems, and it is represented as a cloud-shaped symbol.

    C. An activity partition is a group of related activities that share the same resources or characteristics, and it is represented as a vertical swimlane.

    D. An activity partition is a specialized type of object used for data storage, and it is represented as a cylinder.

Answers

1. A
2. D
3. A
4. C
5. D
6. C

5

Designing a Secure System Model

Designing a secure system model is critical to building a secure software application or IT infrastructure. The system model defines the architecture and structure of your entire system, including hardware, software components, networks, and data flows.

In this chapter, we're going to cover designing a secure system model by looking at the following main topics:

- Partitions
- Modeling interactions between partitions
- UML component diagrams
- Adding swim lanes to UML activity diagrams
- Patterns
- Example of the enterprise secure system model

Partitions

Partitions in a system model, often called system partitions or system decomposition, involve breaking down a complex system into smaller, more manageable components or subsystems. These partitions help understand, design, and organize a system's architecture. Partition boundaries are also where most software security risks exist because the boundary naturally has data passing across it to get to the next partition in the architecture. In this chapter, we will explore different architectural styles that utilize the partitions differently.

Here's how partitions are typically used in a system model:

- **Divide and conquer**: Partitioning allows you to divide a complex system into smaller, self-contained parts. Each partition or subsystem can be designed, developed, and tested independently, making it easier to manage the system as a whole.

- **Separation of concerns**: Partitioning enables the separation of different concerns or aspects of the system. For example, you can partition a software system into modules responsible for user interface, business logic, and data storage. This separation makes it easier to focus on each aspect without being overwhelmed by the complexity of the entire system.

- **Hierarchical structure**: Systems can have multiple levels of partitions, creating a hierarchical structure. This hierarchical decomposition helps us understand how higher-level subsystems are composed of lower-level components, providing a clear structure for the system.

- **Encapsulation and abstraction**: Partitions can encapsulate related functionality and data into a single component. This encapsulation promotes abstraction, where you can hide the internal details of a partition and provide a well-defined interface. By hiding the internal details, modifications in the partition cause less of a ripple effect of changes in other partitions. As we have discussed and will continue to see throughout this book, change is the enemy of security due to the mistakes often made by implementing the change.

- **Subsystem collaboration**: Partitions define the boundaries within which subsystems or components collaborate. They specify how different system parts interact, communicate, and share data or functionality.

- **Reduced complexity**: Breaking a system into partitions reduces its complexity. Each partition can be designed and understood more quickly than the entire system. This simplification aids in system comprehension, development, and maintenance. This is a reiteration of divide and conquer from a slightly different perspective.

- **Independent development**: Partitioning facilitates concurrent and independent development. Teams or developers can work on different partitions simultaneously without significant dependencies if the interfaces and contracts between partitions are well-defined.

- **Reuse**: Well-designed partitions can be reused in other systems or projects. By partitioning a system with reusability in mind, you can build a library of modular components used in various contexts.

- **Testing and validation**: Testing and validation are more manageable when dealing with partitions. Each partition can be tested individually, and integration testing focuses on the interactions between partitions.

- **Scalability**: Partitions can be added or removed to accommodate changes in system requirements or to handle increased workloads. Scalability is facilitated when the system is designed with a partitioned architecture.

- **Documentation and communication**: Partitions help document and communicate the system's architecture. System models, diagrams, and documentation can be structured around the defined partitions, making it easier for stakeholders to understand and discuss the system's structure and behavior.

Partitioning is a crucial aspect of system design and modeling, and it plays a significant role in organizing, managing, and maintaining complex systems. It helps break down large, intricate systems into manageable parts, making it easier to develop, analyze, and evolve software and hardware systems.

Modeling interactions between partitions

Modeling interactions between partitions in a system is essential for understanding how different subsystems or components collaborate to achieve the system's overall functionality. It helps design, visualize, and document the flow of information and control between other parts of the system.

Here's how you can model interactions between partitions:

- **System decomposition**: Start by identifying and defining the partitions or subsystems in your system. Each partition represents a distinct functional unit, and it may have its own set of responsibilities and capabilities.

- **Use case diagrams**: Create use case diagrams to depict the interactions between the partitions and external actors. Use cases represent specific interactions or functionalities that partitions provide. Actors can be users, other systems, or external entities interacting with the system.

- **Sequence diagrams**: Use sequence diagrams to illustrate the chronological .pngorder of messages and method calls exchanged between partitions during specific scenarios or use cases. Sequence diagrams show how control and data flow from one partition to another.

- **Activity diagrams**: Use activity diagrams to model the flow of the program and the data in a process from start to finish, adding swimlanes to illustrate the program and data flow across partitions in the application.

- **Collaboration diagrams (communication diagrams)**: Collaboration diagrams can visualize the relationships and interactions between partitions. They emphasize the structural aspects of interactions, showing how objects (representing partitions) are connected and communicate.

- **Interface contracts**: Define clear and well-documented interface contracts for each partition. These contracts specify the methods, messages, data formats, and behavior that each partition expects from others when interacting. Interface contracts serve as agreements for inter-partition communication.

- **State diagrams**: In cases where partitions have internal states, state diagrams can be used to model how partitions transition between states and how events or conditions trigger these transitions.

- **Component diagrams**: Component diagrams can represent the physical or logical deployment of partitions within the system. They show how partitions are distributed across hardware or software components and how they are interconnected.

- **Data flow diagrams (DFDs)**: DFDs help model data flow between partitions. They depict data sources, data processes within partitions, and data destinations, helping to understand data exchange between partitions.

- **Message formats**: Specify the formats and protocols for messages and data exchange between partitions. Ensure that all partitions understand and adhere to these formats, making communication more predictable and robust.

- **Error handling**: Model how partitions handle errors, exceptions, and failure conditions. Define how errors are reported and how the system reacts to exceptional situations during inter-partition communication.

- **Testing and validation**: Develop test cases that validate the interactions between partitions. Test scenarios should cover both routine and exceptional situations. Testing helps ensure that partitions work together as expected.

- **Documentation**: Document the interactions between partitions. This documentation should include descriptions of use cases, sequence diagrams, interface contracts, message formats, and any constraints or rules governing inter-partition communication.

Modeling interactions between partitions is a crucial step in system design and architecture. It helps ensure that the system's components work together seamlessly and that the overall system behavior meets the intended requirements. You can create a robust and maintainable system by visualizing and documenting these interactions.

UML component diagrams

A **Unified Modeling Language** (UML) component diagram is a structural diagram that provides a high-level overview of the components, their relationships, and the organization of a system or application. Component diagrams depict the physical or logical components that make up a software system and how these components interact with each other to provide system functionality.

Here are the key elements and conventions of a UML component diagram:

- **Component**: Components are modular units representing a physical or logical system part. Components can be software modules, libraries, hardware devices, or more extensive subsystems. Each component is typically represented as a rectangle with the component name inside. *Figure 5.1* shows the UML component notation.

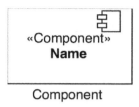

Component

Figure 5.1 – UML component notation

Interface: Interfaces define the services, methods, or operations that a component provides or requires. Interfaces are shown as small rectangles labeled with the interface name. They connect to components through provided (realized) and required interfaces. This is the same for all interfaces we have seen with other UML diagrams.

- **Dependency relationship**: Dependency lines, shown as dashed arrows, represent relationships between components. A dependency indicates that one component relies on another, and a change in the dependent component may affect the dependent component. This is the same for all dependency relations we have seen with other UML diagrams.

- **Provided interface**: A provided interface is associated with a component to indicate the services or functionality that the component offers to other components. *Figure 5.2* shows the provided interface notation.

Provided
Interface

Figure 5.2 – UML provided interface notation

- **Required interface**: A required interface represents the services or functionality `Vdst that a component expects from other components. *Figure 5.3* shows the required interface notation.

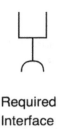

Required
Interface

Figure 5.3 – UML required interface notation

- **Assembly relationship**: An assembly relationship, depicted by a solid line with a solid diamond arrowhead, shows how components are composed to create a more extensive system. It indicates that one component is part of another.

  Realization relationship: A realization relationship, depicted by a dashed line with a solid arrowhead, signifies that a component realizes an interface, which defines how it fulfills its contractual obligations. This is the same for all realization relations we have seen with other UML diagrams.

- **Artifact**: Artifacts are physical files or objects associated with a component. They can represent source code, binaries, configuration files, or other tangible assets. Artifacts are shown as small rectangles attached to components.

- **Package**: Packages are used to group related components, providing a way to organize the diagram when dealing with complex systems. Packages are represented as large rectangles that contain components. This is the same for all packages we have seen with other UML diagrams.

- **Annotations**: Annotations and notes can be added to the diagram to provide additional information about components, interfaces, and relationships.

Here's a simplified example of a UML component diagram for a simple software system:

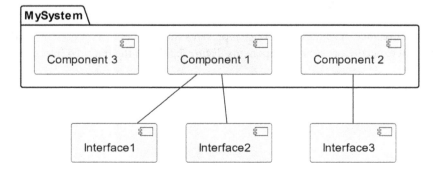

Figure 5.4 – UML component diagram for a simple software system

Let's go through this example:

- `MySystem` is the top-level system
- It contains three components: `Component 1`, `Component 2`, and `Component 3`
- Each component is associated with one or more interfaces that represent the services they provide or require

UML component diagrams help visualize the architecture of a system, illustrating how components work together and aiding in the understanding and communication of system structure. They are beneficial when dealing with complex software or hardware systems.

Patterns

Patterns in system modeling refer to the application of established design patterns to address common architectural and structural challenges in the design and development of complex systems. These design patterns, often derived from software engineering, provide proven and reusable solutions to recurring problems. Applying patterns in system modeling helps improve the system's quality, maintainability, and scalability.

Here are some common patterns used in system modeling:

- **Layered architecture pattern**: This pattern divides the system into multiple layers, each with a specific responsibility. Layers communicate with adjacent layers using defined interfaces. Common layers include presentation, business logic, and data access layers. Many other patterns are implementations of the layered architecture. The architecture in our example ticketing application is three-tiered, with the layers being the web browser, web server, and database server. *Figure 5.5* shows a three-tier pattern where the web browser can make calls to the next layer (the server), which can make calls to the third layer (the database).

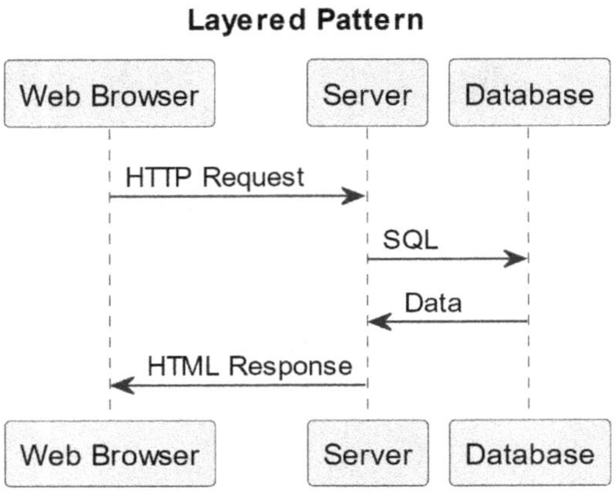

Layered Pattern

Web Browser   Server   Database

HTTP Request

SQL

Data

HTML Response

Web Browser   Server   Database

Figure 5.5 – Layered three-tier pattern

- **Client-server pattern**: In a client-server pattern, the system is split into two parts: the client, which handles the user interface and user interactions, and the server, which manages data storage and processing. This pattern is typical in distributed systems developed in the 80s and 90s. *Figure 5.6* shows the client-server pattern, where multiple clients send requests to the same server and receive responses to their requests.

Client Server Pattern

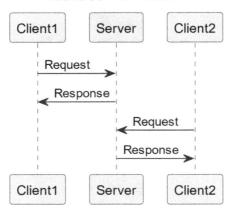

Figure 5.6 – Client-server pattern

- **Microservices architecture**: The architecture decomposes a system into small, independently deployable services. Each service focuses on a specific functionality and communicates through well-defined **Application Programming Interfaces (APIs)**. This pattern promotes scalability and ease of maintenance. *Figure 5.7* shows a model of the microservices pattern. `Service A`, `B`, and `C` are the `Microservices` package components. Arrows represent communication between microservices. For example, `[Service A] --> [Service B]` indicates that `Service A` sends a request to `Service B`.

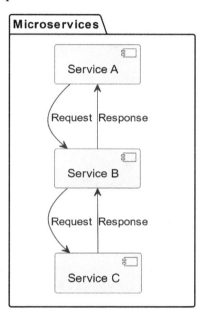

Figure 5.7 – Microservices pattern model

Publish-subscribe pattern: In this pattern, system components can subscribe to events or messages published by other components. It is commonly used for building event-driven and real-time systems. In *Figure 5.8*, a UML class diagram models the publish-subscribe pattern. In this model, `Publisher` is an interface for managing subscribers. `ConcretePublisher` is a class that implements the `Publisher` interface and maintains the state. It notifies subscribers when the state changes. `Subscriber` is an interface for subscribers. `ConcreteSubscriber1` and `ConcreteSubscriber2` implement the `Subscriber` interface and define the behavior when the publisher notifies them. A state can be any information, such as a sensor change in value or a notification of an activity.

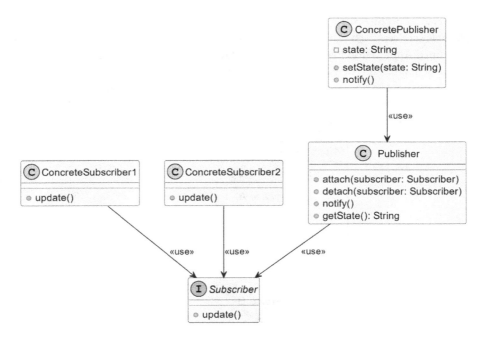

Figure 5.8 – Publish-subscribe pattern

- **Model-View-Controller (MVC) pattern**: MVC separates a system into three main components: the model (data and business logic), the view (presentation and user interface), and the controller (handles user input and controls the flow between the model and view). The MVC pattern is so popular that specific icons were developed to be used in the models, as shown in *Figure 5.9*. In the figure, the images used above the labels model, view, and controller are the standard images. In an actual diagram, the labels would represent the class names, not the labels for the MVC components.

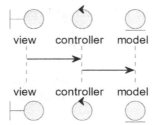

Figure 5.9 – Icons for MVC

- **Pipe and filter pattern**: The pipe and filter pattern divides a system into a series of filters connected by pipes. Data flows through the filters sequentially, and each filter performs a specific transformation or processing step. The Bash shell in Linux is a pipe and filter architecture, allowing you to take the output of a command (filter) and pipe the output as input into another command (filter).

An example Bash command utilizing the pipe and filter is as follows:

```
ls -l|grep "cats"
```

In this example, the `ls` command sends the directory to `grep`, which will filter for files with the word `cat`.

- **Component-based architecture**: In this pattern, a system comprises reusable, self-contained components that encapsulate functionality. Components communicate through defined interfaces, which can be replaced or extended without affecting other system parts. *Figure 5.10* shows a model of the component-based architecture pattern. The `Application` package contains three components: `User Interface`, `Controller`, and `Service`. The `Controller` component communicates with the `Service` component. The `Service` component interacts with the `Repository` component, representing the data access layer. The `Repository` component is associated with the `Database` component, indicating that it interacts with a database.

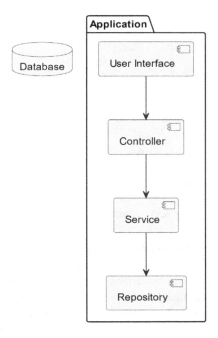

Figure 5.10 – Component-based architecture pattern

- **Service-oriented architecture (SOA)**: SOA structures a system as a collection of loosely coupled services. Services expose well-defined interfaces and can be composed to create more complex functionality. It promotes reusability and interoperability. SOA is a layered architecture but with many more layers than the three-tier presented in *Figure 5.5*.

- **Event-driven architecture**: In an event-driven architecture, components react to events or messages asynchronously. This pattern is commonly used for systems that handle real-time or asynchronous processing. The model presented in *Figure 5.4* is a form of event-driven architecture. In that figure, the external event comes from the publisher. In an event-driven architecture, the event can come from an external event such as a sensor or a user, such as in a graphical user interface.

- **Master-slave pattern**: The master-slave pattern designates one component (the master) to coordinate the activities of other components (the slaves). The master controls and distributes tasks to the slaves. *Figure 5.11* shows a model for the master-slave pattern. The Master Node package contains a single component called Master. The Slave Nodes package contains three components: Slave1, Slave2, and Slave3. Arrows represent communication from Master to each Slave component, indicating that Master Node directs or controls Slave Nodes.

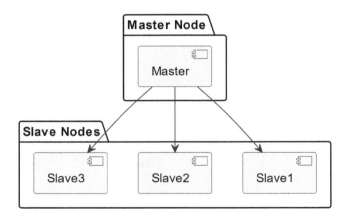

Figure 5.11 – Master-slave pattern

- **Proxy pattern**: The proxy pattern involves creating a surrogate or placeholder object to control access to another object. It is often used to add functionality, such as lazy loading or access control. We will often use the proxy pattern to control access to data and services for each partition. *Figure 5.12* shows a model of the proxy pattern. Subject is the interface that both RealSubject and Proxy implement. RealSubject is the real object that performs the actual work. Proxy is the proxy object that controls access to the real subject. It has a reference to RealSubject. Then, Proxy forwards the request to RealSubject when necessary.

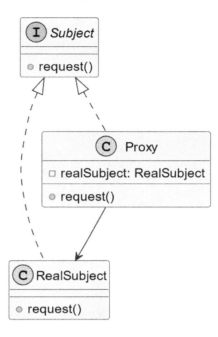

Figure 5.12 – Proxy pattern

- **Adaptive systems pattern**: Adaptive systems adjust their behavior based on changing conditions. They can include feedback loops to monitor system performance and make real-time adjustments.

- **Repository pattern**: The repository pattern provides a consistent and abstract way to access data storage and retrieval. It separates the data access logic from the rest of the system. *Figure 5.13* shows a model of the repository pattern. `Client` represents the application component that interacts with the data. `Repository` is the component responsible for abstracting the data access logic. `Entity` represents the data model or domain entity that the repository works with. The arrow from `Client` to `Repository` indicates that the client interacts with the repository to perform data-related operations, such as querying or saving data. The arrow from `Repository` to `Entity` indicates that the repository works with domain entities.

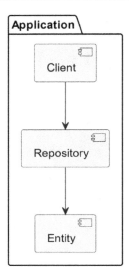

Figure 5.13 – Repository pattern

- **Singleton pattern**: The singleton pattern ensures that a class has only one instance and provides a global access point to that instance. It's often used for managing global resources or configurations. A UML class diagram demonstrating a singleton class is provided in *Figure 5.14*. The `getInstance` method is used instead of the constructor to get a reference to the single instance of the class.

Singleton

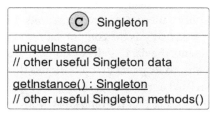

Figure 5.14 – Singleton class

Applying these patterns in system modeling can lead to more efficient, maintainable, and flexible designs. Each pattern addresses specific challenges and best practices, and choosing the correct pattern for your system depends on the system's requirements and architecture. An example you will see throughout this book is a layered *n*-tier architecture used in the example ticketing application. We will apply other patterns for increased security and increased concurrency.

Example – developing an enterprise secure system model

Throughout this book, we will build a secure design for an event ticketing system.

Envision a software system that allows a box office or a website to sell tickets to a famous musical concert or theatre event.

We modify our earlier activity diagram by adding swimlanes to separate the partitions in *Figure 5.15*. Swimlanes are useful in activity diagrams, as you can see when messages cross partition boundaries.

In this example, we have three partitions: the web browser, the web server, and the database server. Vulnerabilities often exist when messages are passed across the partition boundaries.

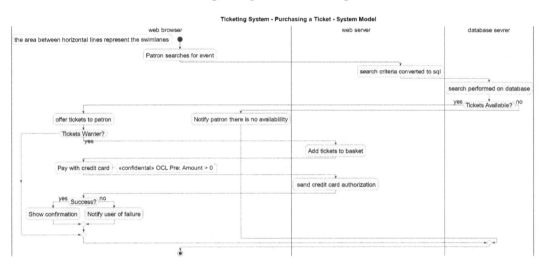

Figure 5.15 – Activity diagram with swimlanes

In *Figure 5.16*, we introduce a component model that shows the same three components from the preceding activity diagram swimlanes and a few interfaces supported by the components.

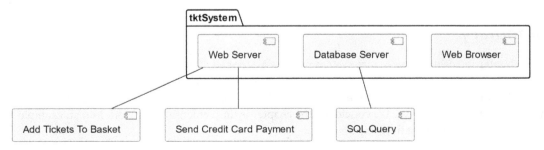

Figure 5.16 – Ticketing system component model

Figure 5.17 enhances our earlier sequence diagram (*Figure 4.3* in *Chapter 4*) by implementing the proxy pattern. A boundary object that we call the dispatcher is added to the model to provide a layer of abstraction between the patron and the objects in the system.

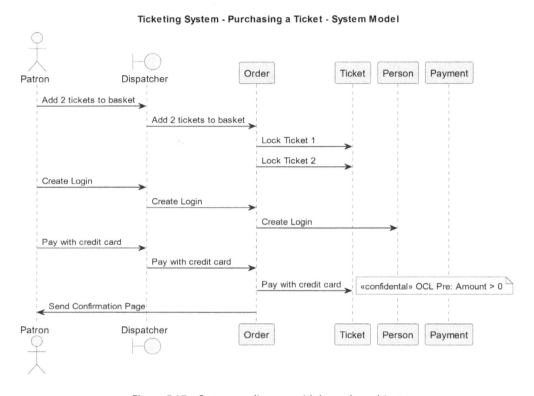

Figure 5.17 – Sequence diagram with boundary object

Comparing the new sequence diagram (*Figure 5.4*) and the new activity diagram (*Figure 5.2*), the objects behind the dispatcher all exist in the web server partition from the activity diagram.

Summary

This chapter introduced the secure system model. We looked at partitioning our application into separate units that communicate together. Next, we looked at patterns in software development that can assist with our system model. We introduce UML component diagrams to model the partitions and their external interfaces. We concluded the chapter by implementing our work into an example system model for an event ticketing system.

The next chapter will look at building threat models to represent the vulnerabilities in our application's dynamic activity.

Self-assessment questions

1. What is high coherence?

    A. A change in one subsystem will not affect any other subsystem

    B. Changes to one subsystem will have a high impact on the other subsystem

    C. Lots of miscellaneous and auxiliary classes, and almost no associations

    D. The classes in the subsystem perform similar tasks and are related to each other via many associations

2. What is low coherence?

    A. The classes in the subsystem perform similar tasks and are related to each other via many associations

    B. Lots of miscellaneous and auxiliary classes, and almost no associations

    C. Changes to one subsystem will greatly impact the other subsystem

    D. A change in one subsystem will not affect any other subsystem

3. What is low coupling?

    A. The classes in the subsystem perform similar tasks and are related to each other via many associations

    B. Lots of miscellaneous and auxiliary classes, and almost no associations

    C. Changes to one subsystem will have a high impact on the other subsystem

    D. A change in one subsystem will not affect any other subsystem

4. What is high coupling?

    A. The classes in the subsystem perform similar tasks and are related to each other via many associations.

    B. Lots of miscellaneous and auxiliary classes, and almost no associations

    C. Changes to one subsystem will have a high impact on the other subsystem

    D. A change in one subsystem will not affect any other subsystem

5. Which architectural style consists of two subsystems called pipes and filters?

    A. Repository architecture

    B. Pipes and filters architecture

    C. MVC architecture

    D. Three-tier architecture

Answers

1. D
2. B
3. D
4. C
5. B

6
Threat Modeling

Threat modeling systematically identifies and evaluates potential security threats and vulnerabilities in a software application, system, or network. It is a proactive security technique used to understand and address security risks during the design and development stages. Threat modeling aims to reduce the likelihood and impact of security breaches by identifying and mitigating potential threats early in the development process.

In this chapter, we're going to cover threat modeling by looking at the following main topics:

- Threat model overview
- STRIDE
- DREAD
- Attack trees
- Mitigations
- Microsoft threat modeling
- Example of the enterprise threat model

By the end of this chapter, you will understand how and why we use threat models. You will also have had exposure to several thread modeling frameworks.

Threat model overview

Software threat modeling is a systematic approach to identifying and mitigating potential security threats in a software application. The goal is to proactively identify and address security vulnerabilities before deploying the software. Threat modeling helps developers, architects, and security professionals understand the potential risks to a system and implement appropriate security controls. Here is an overview of the critical steps involved in software threat modeling:

1. Define the scope:

   - Clearly define the boundaries and components of the system you are analyzing.

   - Identify the assets, such as sensitive data or critical functionality, that need protection.

   - The function design phase we discussed in *Chapter 2* addresses this step.

2. Create a system overview:

   - Develop high-level diagrams of the system architecture.

   - Identify the main components, interfaces, and data flows within the system.

   - The object, dynamic, and system design phases we discussed in the previous chapters address this step. We discussed object design in *Chapter 3*, dynamic design in *Chapter 4*, and system design in *Chapter 5*.

3. Identify threats:

   - Enumerate potential threats and vulnerabilities that could affect the security of the system.

   - Consider various attack vectors, including unauthorized access, data breaches, denial-of-service attacks, and more.

   - Identify common threats by using threat intelligence, historical data, and security best practices. You should familiarize yourself with security standards and best practices, such as those outlined by NIST and ISO.

4. Identify assets and attack surfaces:

   - Clearly define the assets that need protection, such as sensitive data, user accounts, or critical system components.

   - Identify potential attack surfaces where adversaries could exploit vulnerabilities to compromise the system.

5. Determine threat actors:

- Identify potential threat actors or personas that might target the system.

- Consider internal and external threats, including attackers with different motivations and skill levels – for example, a disgruntled worker versus a state agency such as China or Russia.

6. Risk assessment:

- Evaluate the potential impact and likelihood of each identified threat.

- Prioritize threats based on the level of risk they pose to the system. For example, if one threat has a high likelihood, we should allocate resources to reduce the risk versus a low-likelihood threat.

7. Mitigation strategies:

- Develop and implement mitigation strategies for each identified threat. In later chapters, we will drill into several mitigation strategies, such as authentication and authorization controls, activity logging, data redundancy, constraints, and so on.

- Consider security controls, best practices, and design changes to address vulnerabilities.

- Strive for a balanced approach that includes both preventive and detective controls. You cannot predict all vulnerabilities, and you want to ensure you allocate resources to detect things that go wrong you did not anticipate.

8. Validate and iterate:

- Validate the effectiveness of the proposed mitigations through testing and validation activities.

- Iterate the threat modeling process as the system evolves or new information becomes available.

9. Documentation:

- Document the threat model, including identified threats, assets, attack surfaces, and mitigation strategies.

- Ensure the documentation is accessible to relevant stakeholders and can be updated as needed.

10. Integrate into SDLC:

- Integrate threat modeling into **the software development lifecycle (SDLC)** to ensure it becomes a routine part of the development process.

By systematically following these steps, organizations can enhance the security of their software applications and reduce the likelihood of security breaches. Threat modeling is a proactive approach that helps identify and address potential security issues early in development, saving time and resources in the long run. *Figure 6.1* shows some statistics from cloudwards.net that show how large these cybersecurity issues are for folks who build and use software. You can hopefully see why it is essential to utilize the threat modeling methodology to find potential vulnerabilities early so the risks of a breach can be reduced.

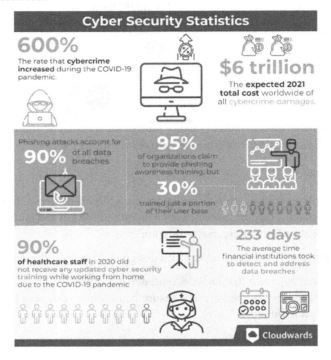

Figure 6.1 – Cybersecurity Statistics from cloudwards.net

The STRIDE threat model

The STRIDE model is the predominant threat modeling technique used in software development today. The STRIDE model is a framework for identifying and categorizing different security threats affecting a system. Developed by Microsoft, **STRIDE** stands for **Spoofing**, **Tampering**, **Repudiation**, **Information Disclosure**, **Denial of Service**, and **Elevation of Privilege**. Each of these represents a category of threats that could potentially compromise the security of a system. Let's explore each element of the STRIDE model:

- Spoofing:

  - Description: Spoofing involves an attacker pretending to be someone else. Attacks of this sort could include impersonating a user, device, or system component.

  - Example: A malicious user gaining unauthorized access to a system using someone else's credentials.

- Tampering:

  - Description: Tampering threats involve unauthorized data modification, code, or system components.

  - Example: An attacker alters the contents of a database to manipulate information or disrupt the system's regular operation.

- Repudiation:

  - Description: Repudiation threats involve denying actions or events by a user or system entity.

  - Example: A user performing a critical action in a system and then denying having taken that action, making it challenging to attribute responsibility.

- Information disclosure:

  - Description: Information disclosure threats involve exposing sensitive information to unauthorized individuals or systems.

  - Example: Unauthorized access to confidential data, such as customer records or financial information.

- Denial of Service (DoS):

  - Description: DoS threats aim to disrupt or degrade the availability of a system or its components, making them inaccessible to legitimate users.

  - Example: Overloading a web server with a flood of requests to the point where it becomes unresponsive to legitimate users.

- Elevation of privilege:

  - Description: Elevation of privilege threats involve an attacker gaining higher access or permissions than authorized ones.

  - Example: Exploiting a vulnerability to escalate user privileges from a regular user to an administrator.

When applying the STRIDE model, security professionals and developers can systematically analyze a system to identify potential threats in each category. This analysis can be part of the threat modeling process, helping to assess and mitigate risks. By understanding the specific types of threats a system may face, appropriate security controls and countermeasures can be implemented to protect against them. *Table 6.1* shows an example of a simple STRIDE model for a software system. The rows represent methods that are exposed across partitions. The Xs in the cells represent where vulnerabilities exist.

Function	S	T	R	I	D	E
Method 1	X		X		X	X
Method 2		X			X	
Method 3					X	X
Method 4	X	X	X		X	
Method 5	X	X			X	

Table 6.1 – Example STRIDE model

It's worth noting that STRIDE is often used with other threat modeling methodologies and tools to understand security risks in a given system comprehensively.

The DREAD threat model

DREAD is another threat modeling framework that helps assess and prioritize security risks associated with a software application. **DREAD** stands for **Damage, Reproducibility, Exploitability, Affected Users**, and **Discoverability**. Here's a brief overview of each component in the DREAD model:

- Damage:

  - Description: Damage assesses the potential impact of a security vulnerability if it were to be exploited. The damage includes considering the extent of harm that could be caused to the organization, its users, or its assets.

  - Scoring: Typically scored on a scale from 0 to 10, where 0 indicates no damage, and 10 indicates catastrophic damage.

- Reproducibility:

  - Description: Reproducibility evaluates how easily an attacker can reproduce the conditions necessary to exploit a vulnerability. A vulnerability that is easily reproducible is considered more serious.

  - Scoring: Scored on a scale from 0 to 10, where 0 means the vulnerability is difficult or impossible to reproduce, and 10 means it is effortless.

- Exploitability:

  - Description: Exploitability measures how easily an attacker can exploit a vulnerability. The exploitability considers factors such as the complexity of the attack and the skills required to carry it out.

- Scoring: Scored on a scale from 0 to 10, where 0 indicates the vulnerability is difficult or impossible to exploit, and 10 means it is effortless.

- Affected users:

  - Description: Affected users involves assessing the number of users or systems that exploiting a vulnerability could impact. The more users affected, the higher the score.

  - Scoring: Scored on a scale from 0 to 10, where 0 means a limited number of users are affected, and 10 means many users are affected.

- Discoverability:

  - Description: Discoverability considers how easy it is for an attacker to discover a vulnerability. A vulnerability is more likely to be exploited if it is easily found.

  - Scoring: Scored on a scale from 0 to 10, where 0 indicates the vulnerability is difficult to discover, and 10 means it is straightforward.

After assessing each factor, a cumulative score is calculated for each vulnerability. The higher the total DREAD score, the higher the priority for addressing that vulnerability. The cumulative score helps organizations prioritize their efforts in addressing security issues based on their potential impact and ease of exploitation. *Table 6.2* displays an example DREAD model. In the model, the rows are methods exposed across partitions.

Function	D	R	E	A	D
Method 1	2	1	8	9	1
Method 2	4	5	9	6	3
Method 3	9	9	9	9	3
Method 4	9	3	9	3	2
Method 5	7	7	4	1	3

Table 6.2 – Example of the DREAD model

DREAD is a simple yet effective model that provides a quantitative approach to threat prioritization. It is often used with other threat modeling methodologies and tools to assess and address security risks in software applications comprehensively.

Attack trees

Attack trees are a graphical representation of potential threats and attacks against a system. They are used in cybersecurity and risk analysis to model and analyze the various ways an attacker might exploit vulnerabilities in a system to achieve a specific goal. Attack trees help visualize and understand the different attack paths adversaries might take. Here's an overview of how attack trees are structured and utilized:

Here are the components of an attack tree:

- **Root node**: Represents the overall goal that an attacker wants to achieve, such as gaining unauthorized access to a system, stealing sensitive data, or disrupting services.

- **Nodes**: Nodes or intermediate nodes represent different stages or steps in the attack path. Each node represents a specific subgoal that an attacker must achieve to reach the ultimate goal.

- **Leaves**: Leaves of the tree represent the actual attack scenarios or techniques that an attacker could use to accomplish a subgoal. These are the lowest-level elements and typically involve specific actions or exploits.

Nodes typically are drawn with rectangles but change when the sub-nodes are combined with AND/OR. *Figure 6.1* and *Figure 6.2* show two simple attack trees with two leaf nodes and a goal. In *Figure 6.1*, both leaf nodes must be accomplished because the goal requires the AND.

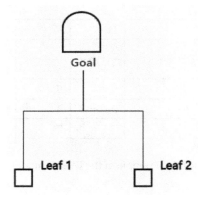

Figure 6.2 – Simple attack tree (AND)

In *Figure 6.3*, either leaf node is enough to get to the goal because of the OR.

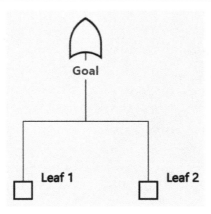

Figure 6.3 – Simple attack tree (OR)

Here are the steps involved in creating an attack tree:

1. Identify the attack objective: Clearly define the overall objective that an attacker aims to achieve. The objective could be, for example, unauthorized access, data exfiltration, or service disruption.

2. Decompose the objective: Break the overall objective into smaller, more manageable subgoals. Each subgoal becomes a node in the attack tree.

3. Identify attack paths: Identify multiple attack paths or scenarios that an attacker might follow to achieve that subgoal for each subgoal. These become branches or paths in the attack tree.

4. Specify attack techniques: Identify and detail the specific techniques or actions an attacker could employ for each attack path. These are represented as leaves in the attack tree.

5. Assign probabilities and impact: Optionally, assign probabilities to branches and estimate the impact of successful attacks. The probabilities help in risk assessment and prioritization of security measures.

What follows is an example of an attack tree:

- Objective: Unauthorized access to a user's email account
- Subgoals:
  - Obtain the user's login credentials
  - Bypass multi-factor authentication

- . Attack paths:

  - User authentication bypass

  - Exploit session management

  - SQL injection

- Attack techniques (leaves):

  - Weak policies

  - Brute force

  - Dictionary attack

  - Session fixation

  - Session hijacking

  - Login form

  - Basket form

Here are some benefits of attack trees:

- Visualization: Attack trees visually represent potential attack paths, making it easier for stakeholders to understand the security risks.

- Risk assessment: They help assess the likelihood and impact of different attack scenarios, aiding in risk management and prioritization of security efforts.

- Security design: Attack trees can be used proactively during the design phase to identify and address potential vulnerabilities before deploying a system.

- Communication: They facilitate communication between security professionals, developers, and other stakeholders by providing a common framework for discussing security risks.

Attack trees are valuable in the broader threat modeling field, helping organizations systematically analyze and address potential security threats in their systems and software. They are terrific at visualizing multi-step attacks. *Figure 6.4* shows a graphical representation of the preceding attack tree.

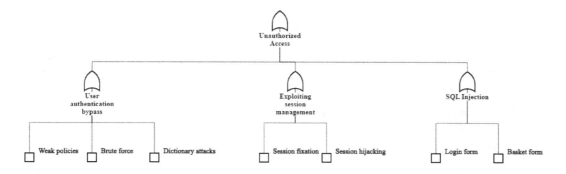

Figure 6.4 – Attack tree

Mitigations

Mitigations in the context of software threat modeling refer to strategies or measures designed to reduce the risk of security threats and vulnerabilities in a software system. Here are common mitigations that can be applied to address various types of threats:

- **Authentication and authorization**: Implement robust authentication mechanisms to ensure only authorized users can access the system. Use role-based access control to limit users' privileges based on their roles.

- **Input validation and sanitization**: Validate and sanitize all user inputs to prevent attacks such as SQL injection or Cross-Site Scripting (XSS). Use parameterized queries and prepared statements in database interactions. We will drill into the details in the mitigation chapters later in the book.

- **Encryption**: Encryption protects sensitive data in transit and at rest. Employ protocols such as HTTPS for secure communication and encrypt sensitive information stored in databases.

- **Secure coding practices**: Train developers in secure coding practices to reduce the likelihood of introducing vulnerabilities. Conduct regular code reviews and use automated tools to identify and fix security issues in the code base.

- **Patch management**: Keep software and dependencies up to date by applying patches and updates regularly. Monitor for security advisories and promptly address known vulnerabilities in third-party libraries.

- **Monitoring and logging**: Implement robust monitoring and logging mechanisms to detect and respond to security incidents. Monitor system logs, network traffic, and user activities to identify potential threats.

- **Error handling**: Implement proper error handling to provide minimal information to users in case of errors. Avoid exposing sensitive details that attackers could exploit.

- **Network security**: Employ firewalls, intrusion detection/prevention systems, and other network security measures to protect against unauthorized access and network-based attacks.

- **Security headers**: Use security headers in web applications to enhance browser security. Headers such as Content Security Policy (CSP), HTTP Strict-Transport-Security (HSTS), and X-Content-Type-Options help mitigate various risks.

- **Threat intelligence**: Stay informed about security threats and vulnerabilities by monitoring threat intelligence sources. This awareness enables organizations to implement mitigations against emerging threats proactively.

- **Data backups**: Regularly back up critical data to ensure recovery during a security incident, such as a ransomware attack. Test backup and restoration processes to verify their effectiveness.

- **Security training and awareness**: Educate users and employees about security best practices. Promote a culture of security awareness to reduce the risk of social engineering attacks and improve the overall security posture.

- **Incident response plan**: Develop and maintain an incident response plan that outlines the steps to be taken during a security incident. Regularly test and update the plan to ensure its effectiveness.

It's important to note that the effectiveness of these mitigations depends on the specific context of the software system and the nature of the threats it faces. A comprehensive approach to security involves a combination of these mitigations tailored to the requirements and risks of the software application. Additionally, organizations should continuously assess and update security measures to adapt to evolving threats.

Microsoft Threat Modeling Tool

Microsoft has done a great job in sharing its threat modeling techniques. Creating a **Data Flow Diagram (DFD)** in Microsoft Threat Modeling is a crucial step. A DFD visually represents the flow of data within a system, helping to identify potential security threats and vulnerabilities. Here's a more detailed breakdown of how Microsoft integrates threat modeling with a DFD:

- Define the system:

  - Understand the architecture and design of the software system.

  - Identify components, processes, and external entities.

- Identify assets:

  - Identify and prioritize assets, including sensitive data, resources, and components.

- Create a DFD:

  - Develop a DFD that illustrates the flow of data through the system.

  - Define processes, data stores, data flows, and external entities.

  - Show how data moves between different components.

- Identify trust boundaries:

  - Identify trust boundaries where the level of trust changes. A simple example is when a message goes from inside a firewall to outside the firewall.

  - These boundaries may separate different security zones within the system.

- Identify threats using a DFD:

  - Analyze the DFD to identify potential threats and vulnerabilities.

  - Consider both technical and non-technical threats.

- Rank and prioritize threats:

  - Prioritize threats based on their potential impact and likelihood.

  - Focus on the most critical threats that need immediate attention.

- Mitigation strategies:

  - Develop mitigation strategies for each identified threat.

  - Modify the DFD to incorporate security controls or changes to the design.

- Review and iterate:

  - Review the threat model, including the DFD, with relevant stakeholders.

  - Iterate on the model based on feedback and additional insights.

- Integrate into the SDLC:

  - Integrate threat modeling with DFD into the software development life cycle (SDLC).

  - Ensure that security considerations are addressed at every stage of development.

- Automate where possible:
  - Use tools such as the Microsoft Threat Modeling Tool to automate parts of the threat modeling process.
  - Automation can help streamline the identification and analysis of potential threats.
- Educate teams:
  - Provide training to development teams on how to use DFDs for threat modeling.
  - Help teams understand the importance of considering security early in the design phase.

By combining the visual representation provided by the DFD with the systematic analysis of potential threats, Microsoft's approach aims to create a comprehensive and actionable threat model. Their methodologies are similar to the techniques presented in this chapter and book. Our methodologies focus more on the source code, whereas Microsoft's focus more on the data. We believe both methods have value and think it is essential to share the Microsoft approach.

Example of an enterprise threat model

Throughout this book, we will build a secure design for an event ticketing system. Envision a software system that allows a box office or a website to sell tickets for a famous musical concert or theatre event. *Table 6.3* is a simplified STRIDE model for our ticketing example. In the model, the login method has all the vulnerability types, while the event selection method has the denial of service vulnerability.

Function	S	T	R	I	D	E
Login	X	X	X	X	X	X
Event Selection					X	
Seat Selection					X	X
Payment	X	X	X		X	
Print at Home	X	X			X	

Table 6.3 – Ticketing STRIDE model

It is important to remember that the rows should be methods in your dynamic models. It is also important to remember that these models are as much an art as a science. One could debate the vulnerabilities I marked in the model. That is the goal. We want to communicate and explore the vulnerabilities early in the process. *Table 6.4* represents the same methods in a DREAD model. The DREAD model shows our understanding of the level of risk by assigning values from one to 10.

Function	D	R	E	A	D
Login	8	1	8	9	1
Event Selection	9	9	9	9	3
Seat Selection	9	9	9	9	3
Payment	9	3	9	3	2
Print at Home	7	7	4	1	3

Table 6.4 – Ticketing DREAD model

We show an attack tree for our example domain in *Figure 6.5*.

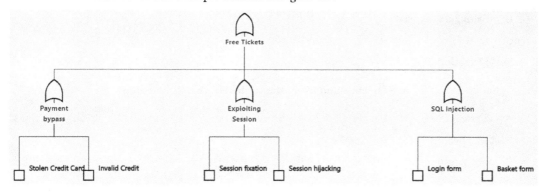

Figure 6.5 - Ticketing attack tree

The model shows that an attacker can get free tickets by bypassing payment, exploiting the session, or performing SQL injection.

Summary

This chapter introduced threat modeling. We looked at STRIDE and threat models that allow us to model threats to methods in our software. Next, we looked at attack trees to enable us to model multi-step attacks against our software. We quickly looked at mitigations we can utilize to reduce risks in our software.

In the next chapter, we drill into implementation in more depth, focusing on mitigations we can implement in our software.

Self-assessment questions

1. What is a threat model?

    A. A type of malware

    B. A cybersecurity certification

    C. A systematic approach to identifying and evaluating potential security threats

    D. A hardware security device

2. What does the first "D" mean in the DREAD threat modeling framework?

    A. Data encryption

    B. Damage potential

    C. Design

    D. Detection

3. What does the "T" in STRIDE stand for in the context of threat modeling?

    A. Time

    B. Tampering

    C. Trespassing

    D. Trust

4. In the STRIDE threat model, what does the "R" represent?

    A. Reliability

    B. Remote execution

    C. Repudiation

    D. Reusability

5. Suppose you are analyzing a potential security breach using an attack tree. In the attack tree, you have identified two possible attack paths to compromise a sensitive database:

    Path 1:

    The attacker gains physical access to the server room.

    The attacker compromises the server hardware.

    The attacker accesses the sensitive database.

Path 2:

The attacker exploits a known software vulnerability on the database server.

The attacker gains unauthorized access to the sensitive database.

Which of the following best describes the attack tree structure for this scenario?

A. A single leaf node that represents the sensitive database with two parent nodes, one for each attack path.

B. A single root node with two leaf nodes representing Path 1 and Path 2.

C. A single root node with three child nodes representing physical access, server compromise, and database access, with appropriate connections.

D. Two separate attack trees, one for Path 1 and one for Path 2.

Answers

1. C
2. B
3. B
4. C
5. C

Part 2: Mitigating Risks in Implementation

The book's second part looks at tools and strategies to reduce the security risks we identified in our earlier models.

This part has the following chapters:

- *Chapter 7, Authentication and Authorization*
- *Chapter 8, Input Validation and Sanitization*
- *Chapter 9, Standard Web Application Vulnerabilities*
- *Chapter 10, Database Security*

7

Authentication and Authorization

Authentication and authorization stand as pivotal security components within software systems, networks, and applications. They play a crucial role in mitigating risks previously identified in the earlier chapters of the software development process. They work together to ensure that the users or entities accessing a system are who they claim to be and that they have the appropriate permissions to perform specific actions.

In this chapter, we're going to cover authentication and authorization by looking at the following main topics:

- Authentication
- Authorization
- Security models
- Single sign-on and open authorization
- Example of enterprise implementation

After completing this chapter, you will be able to differentiate between authentication and authorization, along with having the ability to implement some standard methods for implementing both.

Authentication

Authentication in software systems is a critical security component that involves verifying the identity of users, processes, or systems before granting access to resources or functionalities. When authenticating users, we often use a combination of something only the user would know, something about the user, something the user has, and, potentially, someplace the use is. Here are the key aspects and methods of authentication in software systems:

- **User Authentication – Username and Password**: This is the most common method in which users provide a unique username and a secret password. This form of authentication falls into the category of something only the user should know. Multi-factor authentication (MFA) requires users to provide multiple forms of identification, such as a password and a temporary code sent to their mobile device.

- **Biometric authentication**: There are several methods commonly used in biometric authentication: fingerprint, hand, retina, facial, and voice recognition. This form of authentication falls into the category of something about the user. The system verifies the identity with fingerprint recognition based on unique fingerprint patterns. With hand recognition, the user's stationary hand gesture is used to identify the user. Retina scans utilize up to 400 unique data points in the retina image. With facial recognition, the system authenticates users by analyzing the different facial features of the person being authenticated. With voice recognition, the system validates the user's identity through the user's voice patterns.

- **Token-based authentication**: **Open authorization (OAuth)** is a widely used protocol that enables secure authorization in a standardized way; it is often used for third-party applications. This form of authentication falls into the category of something the user has. JSON web tokens (JWTs) are an alternative that represents a compact, URL-safe means of representing claims between two parties; it is commonly used for authentication and information exchange. Often, these tokens are delivered via mobile phone applications today, but historically, they were specific key code-generating devices.

- **Single sign-on (SSO)**: This allows users to log in once and access multiple systems or applications without re-entering credentials.

- **Certificate-based authentication**: This involves using digital certificates for authentication, often in combination with **public-key infrastructure (PKI)**. **X.509 certificates** are a standard format for public key certificates, which are used to authenticate and establish secure communication between parties over a network, typically the internet. These certificates are a key component of the transport layer security (TLS) and secure sockets layer (SSL) protocols, which are commonly used to encrypt data transmission over networks.

- **Kerberos authentication**: A network authentication protocol that uses tickets to prove the identity of users and services.

- **Smart card authentication**: Users authenticate with a smart card, typically containing a chip that stores authentication information.

- **Time-based one-time passwords (TOTP)**: Users generate one-time passwords that are valid for a short period, often used with MFA. Popular time-based password apps include **Google Authenticator, Authy,** and **Microsoft Authenticator**. These apps are widely supported by various online services and platforms that offer two-factor authentication functionality.

- **Device authentication**: Authenticating devices based on unique identifiers or certificates, commonly used in Internet of Things (IoT) scenarios. Each device has unique identifiers such as its hardware serial number, international mobile equipment identity (IMEI) number (for mobile devices), media access control (MAC) address (for network interface cards), and more. These identifiers can be used to identify the device uniquely. These unique identifiers can be combined with the certificates discussed earlier.

- **Authentication protocols**: Two major authentication protocols are used in the industry today. The first is **security assertion markup language (SAML)**, which is used to exchange authentication and authorization data between parties. The second is **OpenID Connect (OIDC)**, which is an identity layer on top of **OAuth 2.0** that provides user authentication.

- **Secure channels and protocols**: This ensures that authentication data are transmitted securely over encrypted channels (e.g., HTTPS). X.509 certificates are a key component of the transport layer security (TLS) and secure sockets layer (SSL) protocols, which are commonly used to encrypt data transmission over networks.

- **Session management**: Managing user sessions securely to ensure authenticated states are maintained appropriately.

Authentication is a foundational element of security in software systems, and choosing the right authentication methods depends on factors such as the application's requirements, user experience considerations, and the level of security needed for the system. It is often complemented by authorization mechanisms to control access after successful authentication.

Authorization

Authorization in software refers to granting or denying access to specific resources or functionalities within a system. It is a crucial aspect of security that ensures users or entities have the appropriate permissions to perform specific actions or access particular information.

The critical components of authorization in software include the following:

- **Access control**: Access control mechanisms define and enforce policies that determine what actions or resources a user is allowed to access. This involves assigning users roles, permissions, or privileges based on their identity and the context of their request.

- **Authorization policies**: Authorization policies define the rules and conditions under which access is granted or denied. These policies can be based on factors such as user roles, attributes, time of access, and the sensitivity of the data or operation.

- **Roles and permissions**: Users are often assigned roles representing a set of permissions. Roles simplify access control management by grouping users based on their responsibilities. Permissions specify what actions or resources a user with a particular role can access.

- **Audit trails**: In order to enhance security and accountability, systems often maintain audit trails or logs that record details about authorization decisions, including who accessed what resources and when.

- **Token-based authorization**: In modern applications, token-based authorization is commonly used. This involves issuing tokens (such as OAuth tokens) upon successful authentication, including information about the user's permissions. The tokens are then presented with each request, allowing the system to make authorization decisions based on the token's information.

Effective authorization is crucial for protecting sensitive data, preventing unauthorized access, and ensuring the overall security of software systems. It is often implemented at various levels within an application, including the user interface, business logic, and data storage layers.

Security Models

Security models in software systems provide a structured approach to implementing security measures and controls. These models help define how various security aspects, such as confidentiality, integrity, and availability, are enforced within a system. Here are some standard security models:

- **Bell-LaPadula model**: This was developed for military and government systems; it enforces rules to prevent unauthorized access to classified information. It introduces concepts such as "No Read Up, Write Down." The model's primary focus is to ensure the confidentiality of the information or data. This model is commonly used in government and military environments where data confidentiality is critical, such as classified information systems.

- **Biba Integrity model**: This was designed to prevent data corruption and unauthorized modification. It enforces rules such as "No Write Up, Read Down," aiming to maintain the integrity of information. The model's primary focus is to ensure the integrity of the information or data. This model is commonly used in environments where data integrity is paramount, such as financial systems or critical infrastructure.

- **Clark-Wilson model**: The model emphasizes well-formed transactions and the separation of duties. It ensures that data are accessed and modified only through controlled and verified operations. The model's primary focus is to provide the integrity of the information or data. This model is widely used in commercial environments where data integrity and accountability are essential, such as banking systems and e-commerce platforms.

- **Brewer-Nash model**: This describes the trade-offs between distributed systems' consistency, availability, and partition tolerance. Systems can achieve two out of the three aspects at most. This model is also known as the **CAP theorem**. It focuses on the trade-offs between availability, consistency, and partition tolerance.

- **Role-based access control (RBAC):** This assigns roles to users, and permissions are associated with roles. Access is granted based on the user's role, simplifying administration and reducing the risk of unauthorized access. The focus of RBAC is access control. This model is commonly used in enterprise environments, cloud computing platforms, and network infrastructure to manage access to resources efficiently.

- **Mandatory access control (MAC):** This determines access based on security labels and predefined rules set by a system administrator. MAC is commonly used in government and military environments and focuses on access control.

- **Discretionary access control (DAC):** This allows users to control access to their resources. Owners of resources can set permissions for others. DAC is also focused on access control. This model is commonly found in personal computing environments, file systems, and collaboration tools where users have autonomy over their data and resources.

- **Attribute-based access control (ABAC):** This controls access decisions based on attributes associated with subjects, objects, and the environment. Policies are defined using these attributes. ABAC is also focused on access control. This model suits dynamic and complex access control scenarios, such as healthcare systems, IoT environments, and cloud-based applications.

- **Trusted computing base (TCB):** This is a set of components in a system, including hardware, software, and personnel, that must be trusted to maintain security. The TCB is critical for ensuring the system's security. The overall system security is the focus of TCB.

- **Zero-trust security model:** This assumes threats may exist outside and inside the network. Access is not automatically granted based on location; verification is required from everyone trying to access resources. Network security is the focus of the zero-trust model.

- **Defense in depth:** This involves employing multiple layers of security controls to protect against various attacks. It includes measures at the network, application, and data levels. Defense in depth is also focused on network security. This approach utilizes the other models here to implement the different layers.

- **ISO/IEC 27001:** This is an international standard that systematically manages sensitive company information, ensuring its confidentiality, integrity, and availability. This standard focuses on information security management.

Choosing a suitable security model depends on the software system's requirements, threats, and constraints. A combination of models and security measures is often implemented to provide comprehensive protection.

Single sign-on and open authorization

Single sign-on (SSO) and **open authorization (OAuth)** are becoming standards for implementing authentication and authorization. The two are related concepts but serve different purposes in the context of authentication and authorization.

Single sign-on (SSO)

SSO is a mechanism that allows users to log in once and gain access to multiple systems or applications without the need to re-enter credentials. Once authenticated in one application, the user can access other connected applications without needing separate logins.

The key features of SSO are the following:

- User convenience: Users must only remember and enter credentials once.
- Centralized authentication: Authentication is typically handled by an identity provider (IdP), which authenticates users and issues tokens.
- Reduced password fatigue: Users don't need to remember multiple credentials.

Some examples of SSO Protocols are the following:

- Security assertion markup language (SAML)
- OAuth (used for SSO scenarios)
- OpenID Connect (OIDC), which is an identity layer built on top of OAuth 2.0

Open authorization (OAuth)

OAuth is a protocol that enables secure authorization in a standardized way. It allows third-party applications to access user resources (e.g., data and services) on behalf of the user without exposing the user's credentials.

The key features of OAuth are the following:

- Delegated authorization: Users can grant specific permissions to third-party applications without sharing their credentials
- Token-based access: Instead of sharing credentials, OAuth uses tokens (access tokens or refresh tokens) to grant access
- Scopes: Permissions are defined through scopes, specifying the extent of access a third-party application is granted

The roles involved with OAuth are the following:

- Resource owner: The user who grants access to their resources
- Client: The application requesting access to the user's resources
- Authorization server: This is responsible for authenticating the user and obtaining their consent
- Resource server: This hosts the protected resources that the client wants to access

Some example OAuth flows are the following:

- **Authorization code flow**: This flow enhances security by keeping the client credentials (client ID and client secret) confidential during the authorization process. The authorization code flow is suitable for server-side applications where the client's secret can be kept confidential. If the client is a mobile or native application, the authorization code with a proof key for code exchange (PKCE) is often recommended for enhanced security.

- **Implicit flow**: Implicit flow simplifies the process for client-side applications but comes with security considerations. The access token is exposed in the URL fragment, which increases the risk of token leakage through browser history or logs. To mitigate this risk, developers should use HTTPS to encrypt communication and consider the use of short-lived tokens. In recent years, there has been a shift towards recommending authorization code flow with PKCE, even for client-side applications, as it provides an additional layer of security without needing a client secret.

- **Client credentials flow**: Client credentials flow is suitable for scenarios where the client is the resource owner requesting access to their resources. It is not meant for scenarios where the client is acting on behalf of a user. Client credentials flow does not involve user authentication and is often used in server-to-server communication where the client acts as its resource owner.

- **Resource owner password credentials flow** (**ROPC**): ROPC flow should be used cautiously and is generally considered less secure than other OAuth flows. This is because the client application needs to handle and store the user's credentials, which introduces potential security risks. Additionally, this flow bypasses some security benefits other flows provide, such as authorization codes. In many cases, using other flows, such as authorization code flow or implicit flow, is recommended, especially for public clients or applications where the client cannot be trusted with the user's credentials. ROPC Flow should be used only when there are strong security and trust relationships between the client and the user.

There is a strong relationship between SSO and OAuth, and they are often used together:

- SSO Using OAuth: OAuth can enable SSO by allowing authentication to be delegated to an external identity provider. OAuth tokens can be used as credentials for SSO, allowing users to access multiple applications seamlessly.

- Combining OAuth and OIDC for SSO: OpenID Connect is an identity layer built on top of OAuth 2.0 and is often used for SSO scenarios. It provides additional features, such as standardized user information retrieval, making it suitable for identity and authentication.

In summary, while SSO focuses on user convenience and centralized authentication, OAuth primarily concerns delegated authorization and secure resource access. The two concepts can be combined to create a seamless and secure user experience across multiple applications.

Implementing SSO and OAuth with Google

Implementing SSO and OAuth with Google involves integrating your application with Google's identity and authentication services. The following general steps are for implementing SSO and OAuth with Google (at the date of writing). Google is notorious for changing things, so when you try to implement SSO, the steps may vary, but the concept should still be the same.

There are several steps to take to implement SSO with Google:

1. Create a Project on **Google Cloud Console**:

    •   Go to the Google Cloud Console (https://console.cloud.google.com/).

    •   Create a new project for your application. Figure 7.1 shows a screenshot of a project creation:

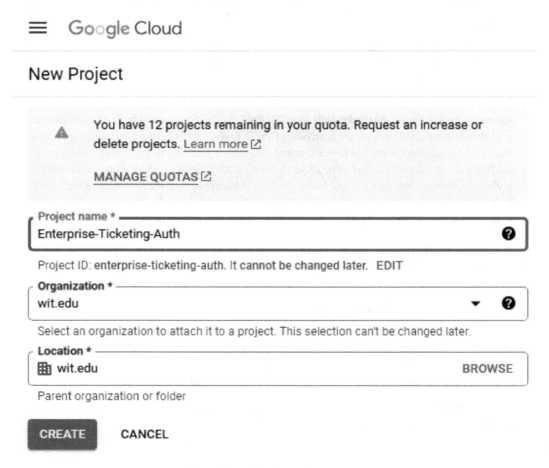

Figure 7.1 – Google project screen

2. Enable Google Identity Platform API:

    - In your project, enable the "Google Identity Platform API" from the API Library. This requires a billing account, but Google will give you a credit to get started. Figure 7.2 shows the setup of the billing account:

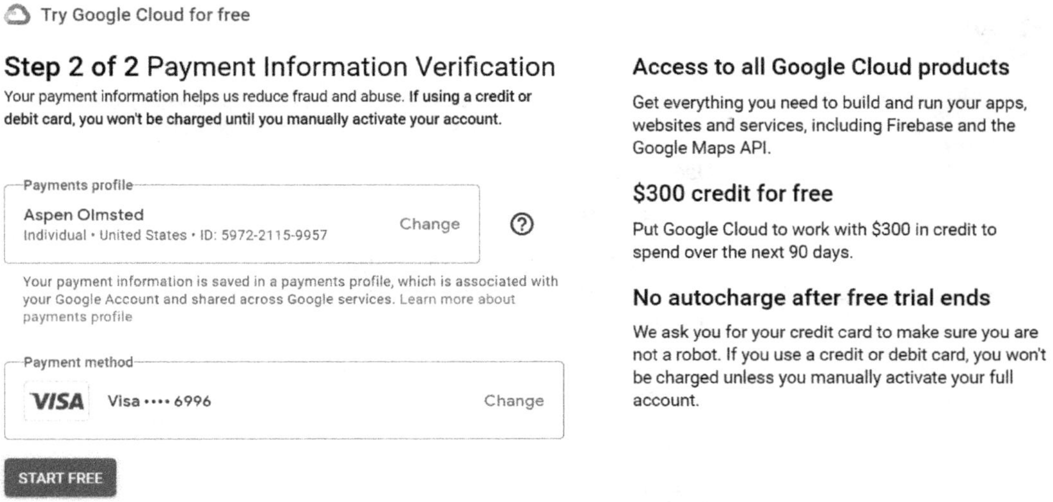

☁ Try Google Cloud for free

Step 2 of 2 Payment Information Verification

Your payment information helps us reduce fraud and abuse. **If using a credit or debit card, you won't be charged until you manually activate your account.**

Payments profile
Aspen Olmsted   Change   ⑦
Individual • United States • ID: 5972-2115-9957

Your payment information is saved in a payments profile, which is associated with your Google Account and shared across Google services. Learn more about payments profile

Payment method
VISA   Visa •••• 6996   Change

START FREE

Access to all Google Cloud products

Get everything you need to build and run your apps, websites and services, including Firebase and the Google Maps API.

$300 credit for free

Put Google Cloud to work with $300 in credit to spend over the next 90 days.

No autocharge after free trial ends

We ask you for your credit card to make sure you are not a robot. If you use a credit or debit card, you won't be charged unless you manually activate your full account.

Figure 7.2 – Setting up a billing account

3. Configure the OAuth consent screen:

    - Set up the OAuth consent screen with the required information about your application. Figure 7.3 shows the setup of the OAuth consent screen:

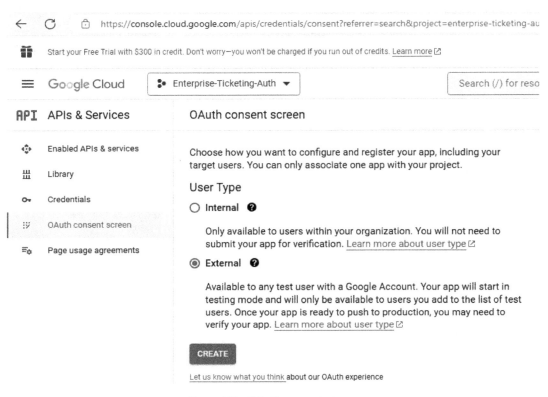

Figure 7.3 – OAuth consent screen

4. Create OAuth credentials:

    -   Generate OAuth client credentials (client ID and client secret) for your application.

    -   Configure the authorized redirect URIs where Google should redirect users after authentication. Figure 7.4 shows the creation of OAuth credentials:

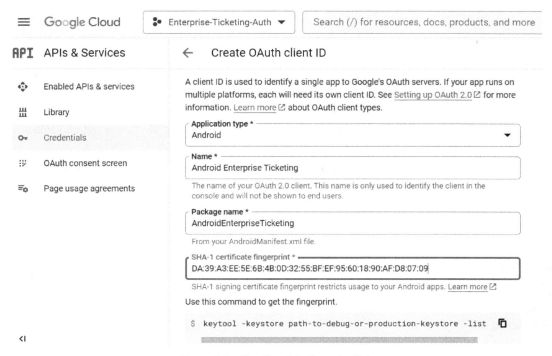

Figure 7.4 – Creating OAuth credentials

5. Integrate Google sign-in SDK:

   - Implement Google sign-in in your application by using the Google sign-in SDK.

   - Use the client ID obtained in the OAuth credentials to initialize the Google sign-in.

6. Handle authentication response:

   - After successful sign-in, handle the authentication response, extract user information, and manage the user session.

There are several steps to implement OAuth with Google (at the time of the writing). The reader may need to reference the latest documentation from Google on implementing OAuth with their web server or application:

1. Choose OAuth flow: Determine the OAuth flow based on your application type (e.g., authorization code flow, implicit flow, etc.).

2. Implement OAuth redirects: Set up redirect URIs in your application to receive the OAuth callback. The following is a sample PHP call to set the redirect:

```
$client->setRedirectUri('https://oauth2.example.com/code');
```

3. Initiate OAuth authorization request: Redirect users to Google's authorization endpoint to initiate the OAuth authorization request. Include the necessary parameters, such as client ID, redirect URI, and scope.

4. User authentication through Google: Users will authenticate with Google and grant the necessary permissions.

5. Handle authorization response: Upon successful authorization, Google redirects users back to your application's specified redirect URI. Extract the authorization code or access a token from the callback.

6. Exchange authorization code for an access token (if applicable): If you are using authorization code flow, exchange the authorization code for an access token by requesting a token from Google's token endpoint.

7. Access Google APIs: Use the obtained access token to access Google APIs on behalf of the user.

Remember to follow Google's guidelines and best practices for secure implementation. Stay informed about any updates or changes to Google's authentication services.

Google provides detailed documentation and guides for implementing SSO and OAuth with various programming languages and platforms, so refer to the specific documentation that aligns with your application stack.

Example of enterprise implementation

Throughout this book, we will build a secure design for an event ticketing system. Envision a software system that allows a box office or a website to sell tickets to a famous musical concert or theatre event. We will implement SSO and OAuth integration to Google for authorization and authentication.

To implement SSO with Google in PHP, you can use OAuth 2.0 and OpenID Connect. Here's a step-by-step guide that worked at the time of this book's publishing. The concepts will still apply when you read this, but Google may change the steps:

1. Create a project in the Google Cloud Console:

   • Go to the Google Cloud Console (https://console.cloud.google.com/).

   • Create a new project or select an existing one.

2. Enable APIs:

   • Enable the "Google+ API" and "Google Identity Toolkit API" for your project.

3. Configure OAuth 2.0 Credentials:

   • Navigate to the "Credentials" page in your Google Cloud Console.

   • Create credentials: OAuth client ID.

- Choose the application type (e.g., web application)
- Set the authorized redirect URI (where Google should redirect after authentication)
- Note the client ID and client secret

4. Install Google API Client Library for PHP from the following command line (other options exist, such as php composer.phar):

```
Php composer.phar require "google/apiclient:~2.0@dev"
```

5. Implement SSO in your PHP application:

- Create a login button in your HTML:

```html
<a href="login.php">Login with Google</a>
```

- Create a login.php page:

```php
<?php
require_once 'vendor/autoload.php';

// Set your Google API credentials
$client = new Google_Client();
$client->setClientId('YOUR_CLIENT_ID');
$client->setClientSecret('YOUR_CLIENT_SECRET');
$client->setRedirectUri('YOUR_REDIRECT_URI');
$client->addScope('email');

// Create the URL to initiate Google login
$authUrl = $client->createAuthUrl();

// Redirect to Google login page
header('Location: ' . filter_var($authUrl, FILTER_SANITIZE_
URL));
exit;
?>
```

- Create a callback.php page:

```php
<?php
require_once 'vendor/autoload.php';

// Set your Google API credentials
$client = new Google_Client();
$client->setClientId('YOUR_CLIENT_ID');
$client->setClientSecret('YOUR_CLIENT_SECRET');
```

```php
$client->setRedirectUri('YOUR_REDIRECT_URI');
$client->addScope('email');

// Process the Google login callback
if (isset($_GET['code'])) {
    $token = $client->fetchAccessTokenWithAuthCode($_
GET['code']);
    $client->setAccessToken($token);

    // Get user information
    $oauth2 = new Google_Service_Oauth2($client);
    $userInfo = $oauth2->userinfo->get();

    // Access user information
    $userId = $userInfo->id;
    $userName = $userInfo->name;
    $userEmail = $userInfo->email;

    // Use user information as needed (e.g., log in the user)
    // ...

    echo "Welcome, $userName!";
} else {
    // Handle error or redirect to login page
    // ...
}
?>
```

6. Test your SSO implementation:

    •   Open your application, click **Login with Google**, and verify that the SSO flow works.

Replace `'YOUR_CLIENT_ID'`, `'YOUR_CLIENT_SECRET'`, and `'YOUR_REDIRECT_URI'` with your Google API credentials. These credentials should be stored in a secure location utilizing the approaches discussed earlier to ensure authentication and access. The above example is simplified so as not to handle situations when the user is already authenticated, is a session management, or if the login fails.

Important note:

This example uses the Google API Client Library for PHP, simplifying the integration process. Ensure that your PHP environment supports the required extensions and configurations.

Summary

This chapter introduces authentication and authorization. We looked at the differences between the functions of authentication and authorization. Next, we looked at two key authentication and authorization strategies in software today: single sign-on and open authorization. We concluded by implementing code in our example that utilizes Google for SSO and OAuth.

In the next chapter, we look at critical mitigations for the risks introduced when we accept input for our software.

Self-assessment questions

1. Which of the following is not a typical authentication factor?

   A. Something you know

   B. Something you want

   C. Something you are

   D. Something you have

2. Authorization applies to which of the following?

   A. Subjects

   B. Everyone

   C. Objects

   D. Those in the room

3. Which of the following is not a discussed biometric technology?

   A. Blood scan

   B. Hand scan

   C. Voice scan

   D. Finger scan

4. What is the primary purpose of role-based access control (RBAC) in authorization?

   A. Verifying user identity through biometrics

   B. Assigning permissions based on user behavior

   C. Restricting access to specific IP addresses

   D. Granting access based on job responsibilities

5.   In the context of access control, what is the principle of least privilege?

   A.   Assigning permissions based on seniority

   B.   Giving users the minimum necessary permissions for their tasks

   C.   Granting users maximum permissions by default

   D.   Providing temporary access to all resources

Answers

   1.   B

   2.   A

   3.   A

   4.   D

   5.   B

8

Input Validation and Sanitization

Input validation and sanitization are critical security measures used in software development to protect applications from a wide range of security vulnerabilities, particularly those related to malicious input or user data. These practices help ensure that the data received by an application is safe, reliable, and free from vulnerabilities that attackers could exploit.

In this chapter, we're going to cover input validation and sanitization by looking at the following main topics:

- Input validation
- Input sanitization
- Language-specific defenses
- Buffer overflows
- Example of enterprise input validation and sanitization

By the end of this chapter, the reader will have a good grasp of how vital validation and sanitation of the input received is in protecting the application.

Input validation

Input validation in software development ensures an application's security, reliability, and robustness. It involves checking and validating the data entered by users or received from external sources to ensure it meets specific criteria before processing. Proper input validation helps prevent security vulnerabilities, data corruption, and other malformed or malicious input issues.

Here are some critical considerations for implementing input validation in software:

- **Data type validation** - Ensure that the input data is of the expected data type (for example, string, integer, date) before processing it. This helps prevent errors and vulnerabilities related to incorrect data types.

- **Length and size checks** - Validate the length and size of input data to ensure it falls within acceptable limits. This prevents buffer overflows, memory issues, and other related vulnerabilities.

- **Format validation** - Check if the input data matches the expected format. For example, validate email addresses, phone numbers, and other data formats to ensure they meet specified patterns. Localization and culture play crucial roles in format validation as different formats are used for dates, currencies, numbers, language, and so on.

- **Range validation** - Verify that numeric input values fall within a defined range. This is important for preventing issues related to out-of-bounds values.

- **Whitelisting versus blacklisting** - Use whitelisting approaches where possible, allowing only known good input rather than blacklisting specific bad inputs. Blacklisting can be error-prone and may not cover all possible malicious inputs.

- **Regular expressions** - Leverage regular expressions to define and enforce patterns for valid input. This is especially useful for validating complex data formats.

- **Error handling** - Use proper error-handling mechanisms to handle invalid input gracefully. Provide informative error messages to users without revealing sensitive information.

- **Client-side and server-side validation** - Implement both client-side and server-side validation. Client-side validation enhances user experience, while server-side validation is essential for security and should not be solely relied upon.

- **Security testing** - Conduct thorough security testing, including penetration testing, to identify and address potential vulnerabilities related to input validation.

By incorporating these best practices, developers can enhance the security and reliability of their software applications. Additionally, staying informed about emerging security threats and regularly updating validation mechanisms help maintain the effectiveness of input validation over time. Adding functionality to turn on logging and monitoring of input can help debug issues and detect abnormal behavior. Our penetration testing chapter will discuss tooling that can help us check for known input validation issues and new threats against input. In many of my commercial projects, we would run nightly scans against websites and public interfaces to see what new known vulnerabilities existed, and the following day, we would work on reducing the risk through input validation.

Input sanitization

Input sanitization is a critical practice in software development aimed at cleaning and validating user inputs to prevent security vulnerabilities and protect against various attacks, such as SQL injection, **cross-site scripting (XSS)**, and other injection attacks. The goal of input sanitization is to ensure that the input data is safe and does not contain malicious code or characters that could compromise the application's security. It is crucial to store data securely once it is input so that it remains sanitized. We will address this in the database security chapter.

Here are fundamental principles and techniques for input sanitization in software development:

- **Filtering and validation** - Filtering removes or disallows any characters or patterns not expected in the input. Validation ensures that the input adheres to expected formats, lengths, and constraints. It is crucial to consider outliers in input that are still valid, such as hyphenated names and other correct but infrequent patterns.

- **Character escaping** - Use character-escaping mechanisms to neutralize or transform special characters with special meaning in a given context. For example, convert characters such as `<`, `>`, `&`, and quotes to their corresponding HTML entities to prevent XSS attacks.

- **Parameterized queries** - When interacting with databases, use parameterized queries or prepared statements to separate user input from SQL code. This helps prevent SQL injection attacks by treating input as data rather than executable code.

- **Whitelisting** - Employ whitelisting strategies to only allow known, safe input. Specify acceptable characters, patterns, or formats, and reject anything else. This approach is often more secure than blacklisting specific dangerous characters.

- **Regular expressions** - Use regular expressions to define and enforce patterns for valid input. This can be particularly useful for complex data formats such as email addresses or phone numbers.

- **URL encoding** - When handling input included in URLs, use URL encoding to replace unsafe characters with percent-encoded equivalents. This prevents issues related to URL manipulation and injection attacks.

- **HTML purification** - If user input is to be displayed as HTML, use HTML purifiers to remove or neutralize any potentially malicious HTML or script tags. This helps prevent XSS attacks by ensuring that only safe HTML is rendered.

- **Input length limitations** - Enforce reasonable limits on input data length to prevent buffer overflows or **denial-of-service (DoS)** attacks. Also, validate and truncate or reject input that exceeds specified length limits.

- **Content Security Policy (CSP)** - Implement CSP headers to control which resources can be loaded and executed. This can mitigate the impact of XSS attacks.

- **File upload security** - File upload security is critical to web application security, as it involves accepting and processing user files. Without proper security measures in place, file upload functionality can be exploited by attackers to upload malicious files, compromise the application, and potentially harm users or the underlying system.

- **Security testing** - Regularly perform security testing, including penetration testing, to identify and address potential vulnerabilities related to input sanitization. Automated tools and manual testing can help identify weaknesses in input handling.

By implementing these practices, developers can significantly enhance the security of their applications and protect against a wide range of common security threats associated with user input. Input sanitization should be an integral part of software development security strategy. As discussed earlier in this chapter, the penetration testing chapter will introduce tooling that can assist us in identifying areas we are not sanitizing input and should. Many historical attacks have been made against websites that do not adequately sanitize input. Many developers have taken up the mantra of *Escape input, do not sanitize*, but escaping (listed previously) is just one of the tools in our toolbox. We need to ensure the output of applications continues to look professional for legitimate users, and escaping can sometimes leave our output looking unprofessional. So, a good balance of the use of approaches is best.

Language-specific defenses

Different programming languages may have specific features and functions to handle input validation and sanitization. Some older and lower-level languages, such as C and C++, require more manual programming to defend against input attacks. Here are language-specific defenses for input validation and sanitization in some commonly used programming languages:

- **Java**:

  - Input validation:

    - Use libraries such as Apache Commons Validator for validating various types of input (for example, emails, URLs, and so on)

    - Leverage regular expressions for complex input validations

  - Input sanitization:

    - Use the **Enterprise Security API** (**ESAPI**) library for input validation and encoding to prevent common security vulnerabilities

    - HTML-encode user inputs when rendering dynamic content in web applications

- **Python**:

  - Input validation:

    - Utilize built-in libraries such as `re` for regular expression-based validation

    - Leverage the `validator` library for validating various types of data (for example, URLs, emails)

  - Input sanitization:

    - Use the `html.escape` function or frameworks such as Django that automatically escape content when rendering templates

    - When dealing with databases, use parameterized queries or **object-relational mapping (ORM)** to prevent SQL injection

- **JavaScript (Node.js)**:

  - Input validation:

    - Use libraries such as `validator.js` for validating strings (for example, `isEmail`, `isURL`)

    - Regular expressions can be employed for custom validations

  - Input sanitization:

    - Use functions such as `encodeURI` and `encodeURIComponent` for URL encoding

    - When working with the DOM, use methods such as `createTextNode` to safely insert text content

- **C# (ASP.NET)**:

  - Input validation:

    - Utilize data annotations for model validation in ASP.NET MVC

    - Regular expressions can be applied using the `Regex` class for custom   validations

  - Input sanitization:

    - HTML-encode output using `HttpUtility.HtmlEncode` or Razor syntax in ASP. NET MVC views

    - Utilize parameterized queries or Entity Framework for database interactions

- **Ruby**:

  - Input validation:

    - Use built-in validation methods such as `String#match` for regular expression-based validation

    - `ActiveRecord` in Ruby on Rails provides model-level validations

  - Input sanitization:

    - Utilize the h helper method or `<%= ... %>` syntax in Rails views to automatically escape HTML

    - Parameterized queries or `ActiveRecord`'s query building can prevent SQL injection

- **PHP**:

  - Input validation:

    - Use functions such as `filter_var` for validating input based on predefined filters

    - Leverage regular expressions for custom validations

  - Input sanitization:

    - Use `htmlspecialchars` or `htmlentities` for HTML encoding

    - Use parameterized queries or **PHP Data Objects** (**PDO**) for secure database interactions to prevent SQL injection

- **Go**:

  - Input validation:

    - Use regular expressions or built-in functions for string validation

    - The `validator` package can be used for more complex validations

  - Input sanitization:

    - Use `html.EscapeString` for HTML encoding

    - When working with databases, use prepared statements to prevent SQL injection

It's important to note that best practices may vary, and developers should always refer to the specific documentation and security guidelines for their programming language and framework. Additionally, maintaining a secure code base is crucial for staying informed about updates and security patches for libraries and frameworks.

Buffer overflows

Buffer overflows are a common type of software vulnerability that occurs when a program writes more data to a buffer (temporary data storage area) than allocated for. This can lead to unpredictable behavior, crashes, and, in some cases, exploitation by attackers to execute malicious code. Defenses against buffer overflows are essential to enhance the security of software applications. Here are some key defenses:

- **Use safe string functions** - Replace standard, non-bounds-checked string functions (for example, `strcpy`, `sprintf`) with their safer counterparts (for example, `strncpy`, `snprintf`) that allow specifying the maximum number of characters to copy.

- **Bounds checking** - Perform explicit bounds checking before copying data into buffers. Ensure that the input data length does not exceed the allocated buffer size.

- **Memory-safe languages** - Choose programming languages that provide memory safety, such as Rust, or languages with memory management mechanisms such as Java or C#. Memory-safe languages help prevent buffer overflows by automatically managing memory allocation and deallocation.

- **Static code analysis** - Employ static code analysis tools to analyze the source code for potential vulnerabilities, including buffer overflows. These tools can identify unsafe coding practices and suggest improvements.

- **Address space layout randomization (ASLR)** - Enable ASLR, a security technique that randomizes the memory addresses used by system components and processes. This makes it more challenging for attackers to predict the location of specific functions or data.

- **Stack canaries** - Use stack canaries, which are random values placed before the return address on a stack. If a buffer overflow occurs, the canary value will likely be overwritten, triggering an alert or terminating the program.

- **Data Execution Prevention (DEP)** - Enable DEP, a security feature that prevents code from executing in specific memory regions. It helps mitigate buffer overflow attacks by making it difficult for attackers to execute injected malicious code.

- **Compiler-based protections** - Enable compiler flags and features that provide additional security, such as `-fstack-protector` for stack canaries and `-D_FORTIFY_SOURCE` to detect specific buffer overflow issues at compile time.

- **Use safe APIs and libraries** - Utilize safe APIs and libraries that perform bounds checking internally and are designed to prevent common programming errors leading to buffer overflows.

- **Regular security audits and testing** - Conduct regular security audits and testing, including penetration testing and fuzz testing, to identify and address potential buffer overflow vulnerabilities. Memory corruption detection tools are essential for identifying and mitigating vulnerabilities in software that can lead to memory-related issues, such as buffer overflows, use-after-free errors, and memory leaks.

- **Code reviews** - Implement thorough code review processes to catch and fix coding errors, including potential buffer overflows, before deploying the software.

- **Sandboxing** - Sandboxing is a technique used to isolate and contain untrusted or potentially malicious code within a restricted environment, known as a sandbox, to prevent it from causing harm to the system or other software components. While sandboxing can help mitigate risks associated with buffer overflows and other memory-related vulnerabilities, it is not specifically designed for testing for buffer overflows. However, sandboxing can be used as part of a comprehensive security testing strategy to identify and prevent buffer overflow vulnerabilities.

- **Control-flow integrity (CFI)** - CFI is a security mechanism designed to prevent attackers from hijacking the control flow of a program and executing arbitrary code. It aims to mitigate control-flow hijacking attacks, such as buffer overflows, **return-oriented programming (ROP)**, and **jump-oriented programming (JOP)**, commonly used by attackers to exploit software vulnerabilities and gain unauthorized access to systems. CFI enforces the integrity of the control-flow graph of a program, ensuring that execution remains within valid control-flow paths defined by the program's intended behavior. It achieves this by instrumenting the program with runtime checks and enforcing strict rules on control-flow transitions. These checks and rules help detect and prevent deviations from legitimate control-flow paths, thwarting control-flow hijacking attacks.

- **Secure coding guidelines** - Adhere to secure coding practices and guidelines, such as those provided by organizations such as the **Computer Emergency Response Team (CERT)** and the **Open Worldwide Application Security Project (OWASP)**. Educate developers on writing secure code and avoiding common pitfalls.

Buffer overflows are usually only an issue with software written in lower-level languages such as C or C++, but many legacy systems have these vulnerabilities. Most homebrew solutions use these vulnerabilities in the gaming console industry to get around the licensing controls. By implementing the defenses itemized in this section, developers can significantly reduce the risk of buffer overflow vulnerabilities in their software applications and enhance overall security. A **defense-in-depth (DID)** approach is essential, combining multiple strategies to create a more robust security posture.

Example of the enterprise input validation and sanitization

Throughout this book, we will build a secure design for an event ticketing system. Envision a software system that allows a box office or a website to sell tickets to a famous musical concert or theatre event. Table 3 is a simplified STRIDE model for our running ticketing example. Next, we will look at utilizing the PHP `filter_var` function and `FILTER_VALIDATE_*` constants to perform input validation for various fields. Here is a PHP code sample that utilizes the `filter_var` extension for validating fields such as `First Name`, `Last Name`, `Phone Number`, `Email`, and `Address`:

```php
<?php

// Function to sanitize and validate input
function sanitize_input($input) {
    $input = trim($input);
```

```php
    $input = stripslashes($input);
    $input = htmlspecialchars($input);
    return $input;
}

// Function to validate name
function validate_name($name) {
    // Name should only contain letters and spaces
    return filter_var($name, FILTER_VALIDATE_REGEXP, array("options"
      => array("regexp" => "/^[a-zA-Z ]*$/")));
}

// Function to validate email
function validate_email($email) {
    // Validate email format
    return filter_var($email, FILTER_VALIDATE_EMAIL);
}

// Function to validate phone number
function validate_phone($phone) {
    // Phone number should only contain numbers, dashes, and
    //parentheses
    return filter_var($phone, FILTER_VALIDATE_REGEXP, array("options"
      => array("regexp" => "/^[0-9\-\(\)]*$/")));
}

// Function to validate address
function validate_address($address) {
    // Basic validation for address (you may need to customize based
    //on your requirements)
    return strlen($address) > 5; // For example, address should be at
                                 //least 6 characters long
}

// Get user input (assuming it comes from a form)
$user_first_name = isset($_POST['first_name'])? $_POST['first_name']:
'';
$user_last_name = isset($_POST['last_name']) ? $_POST['last_
name']:'';
$user_email = isset($_POST['email']) ? $_POST['email']:'';
$user_phone = isset($_POST['phone']) ? $_POST['phone']:'';
$user_address = isset($_POST['address']) ? $_POST['address'] : '';

// Sanitize and validate input
$first_name = sanitize_input($user_first_name);
$last_name = sanitize_input($user_last_name);
```

```
$email = sanitize_input($user_email);
$phone = sanitize_input($user_phone);
$address = sanitize_input($user_address);

// Validate each field
if (!validate_name($first_name)) {
    echo "Invalid First Name format. Please enter a valid name.";
} elseif (!validate_name($last_name)) {
    echo "Invalid Last Name format. Please enter a valid name.";
} elseif (!validate_email($email)) {
    echo "Invalid email address. Please enter a valid email.";
} elseif (!validate_phone($phone)) {
    echo "Invalid phone number. Please enter a valid phone.";
} elseif (!validate_address($address)) {
    echo "Invalid address. Please enter a valid address.";
} else {
    // All input is valid, proceed with further processing
    echo "Input is valid. Processing...";
    // Additional processing logic goes here
}

?>
```

In this example, FILTER_VALIDATE_REGEXP is used with the options parameter to apply regular expression-based validation for the First Name, Last Name, and Phone Number fields. The other fields use built-in constants such as FILTER_VALIDATE_EMAIL for email validation and a simple length check for the address.

When validating customer reviews for an event, we must ensure that the input is safe, free from malicious content, and adheres to specific guidelines. Next is a PHP code sample for input validation for customer reviews using the filter_var extension:

```
<?php

// Function to sanitize and validate input
function sanitize_input($input) {
    $input = trim($input);
    $input = stripslashes($input);
    $input = htmlspecialchars($input);
    return $input;
}

// Function to validate the review content
function validate_review_content($review_content) {
    // Basic validation for review content (you may customize based on
    //your requirements)
```

```
        return strlen($review_content) >= 10; // For example, the review
            should be at least 10 characters long
}

// Get user input (assuming it comes from a form)
$user_review_content = isset($_POST['review_content'])?    $_
POST['review_content'] : '';

// Sanitize and validate input
$review_content = sanitize_input($user_review_content);

// Validate the review content
if (!validate_review_content($review_content)) {
    echo "Invalid review content. Please provide a more detailed
        review.";
} else {
    // All input is valid, proceed with further processing
    echo "Review is valid. Processing...";
    // Additional processing logic goes here
}

?>
```

In this example, the validate_review_content function checks if the review content is at least 10 characters long. The code can easily be adjusted for different length requirements or validation rules can be added based on needs specified earlier in the design process. The example allows blank fields but can easily be extended to check for a zero length. Advanced web services may be used for things such as email, phone numbers, and addresses to add an extra layer of validation.

Summary

This chapter introduced input validation and sanitization. We examined both concepts and how they help ensure our software's safety and robustness. Next, we looked at language-specific defenses that are used to ensure input is protected from malicious attacks. We discussed buffer overflows and strategies to reduce risk.

In the next chapter, we drill into standard web application vulnerabilities and the tools and strategies we utilize to reduce risk.

Self-assessment questions

1. What is the primary purpose of input validation?

    A. Preventing malicious input

    B. Beautifying user interfaces

C. Enhancing user experience

D. Optimizing database performance

2. Which of the following is an example of input validation?

A. Changing the font style based on user input

B. Displaying error messages in red font

C. Allowing only numeric characters in a phone number field

D. Adding animations to form submission buttons

3. Why is input sanitization important in web development?

A. It prevents injection attacks and other security threats

B. It speeds up the loading time of web pages

C. It improves the design of user interfaces

D. It makes the code more readable

4. What is the purpose of escaping user input?

A. Converting special characters to their HTML entities

B. Increasing the font size of user input

C. Making input fields case-insensitive

D. Allowing only uppercase letters in input fields

5. Why is it important to validate and sanitize user input on both the client and server sides?

A. To make the code shorter and more efficient

B. To double-check user input

C. To improve website performance

D. To prevent security vulnerabilities

Answers

1. A
2. C
3. A
4. A
5. D

Standard Web Application Vulnerabilities

Web application vulnerabilities are weaknesses or flaws in the security of web applications that attackers can exploit to compromise the confidentiality, integrity, or availability of data or the application itself. These vulnerabilities can have serious consequences, ranging from data breaches to unauthorized access and code execution.

In this chapter, we're going to cover standard web application vulnerabilities by looking at the following main topics:

- Injection attacks
- Broken authentication and session management
- Request forgery
- Language-specific defenses
- Example of enterprise web defenses

By the end of this chapter, you will have a good understanding of the typical attacks that are made on web applications.

Injection attacks

Injection attacks on web applications refer to malicious attempts to inject or execute unauthorized code or commands into an application's data. These attacks exploit vulnerabilities in the application's input validation mechanisms, allowing attackers to insert malicious code that the application's interpreter then executes. Injection attacks have been around for decades but are successful every day. On the day I wrote this section of the book, I looked for recent attacks and, that week, a threat group named ResumeLooters stole the personal data of over 2 million job seekers after compromising 65 legitimate job listings and retail sites using SQL injection and **Cross-Site Scripting** (**XSS**) attacks. Almost every day, the news is filled with stories like this. Once malicious users are successful, they can use this data or access for further attacks to steal financial assets or cause havoc. The most common types of injection attacks include the following:

- **SQL injection (SQLi)**: Attackers inject malicious SQL statements into input fields, manipulating the database queries executed by the application. This can lead to unauthorized access, data disclosure, and data manipulation.

- **Cross-Site Scripting (XSS)**: Attackers inject malicious scripts (usually JavaScript) into web pages, which are then executed by the victim's browser. This allows attackers to steal user data, hijack sessions, or deface websites.

- **Command injection**: In this attack, attackers inject malicious commands into input fields that are later executed by the system. This can lead to unauthorized access, remote code execution, or other system-level compromises.

- **LDAP injection**: Similar to SQL injection, LDAP injection targets applications that use the **Lightweight Directory Access Protocol** (**LDAP**) for authentication and authorization. Attackers inject malicious LDAP statements to manipulate authentication processes.

- **XPath injection**: XPath is a query language for XML documents. XPath injection involves manipulating XPath queries by injecting malicious code, leading to unauthorized access or disclosure of sensitive information.

To mitigate the risks of injection attacks, software developers should implement secure coding practices, such as the following:

- **Parameterized statements**: Parameterized queries or prepared statements help to ensure that user input is seen as data and not executable code. We will look at this more in the database security chapter.

- **Input validation and sanitization**: Validate and sanitize user input to ensure it matches what is expected and does not contain malicious code. We will explore this more in the chapter dedicated to input validation and sanitization.

- **Least privilege principle**: Limit the permissions of database accounts, web server processes, and other system components to the minimum necessary for their functionality.

- **Web Application Firewalls (WAFs)**: Filter and monitor HTTP traffic between a web application and the internet to identify and block malicious requests.

- **Regular security audits**: Regularly audit and test applications for vulnerabilities, including using penetration testing tools to identify and fix potential injection points.

- **Security headers**: Implementing security headers is crucial in preventing injection attacks such as SQL injection, XSS, and others. These headers help mitigate various attacks by controlling how web browsers interact with your web application. Implementing these security headers can significantly improve the security posture of your web application and help protect against injection attacks and other common web vulnerabilities:

- **Content Security Policy (CSP)**: A CSP allows you to define a whitelist of trusted sources for content such as scripts, stylesheets, images, and fonts. This can help prevent XSS attacks by restricting the sources from which resources can be loaded.

- **X-Content-Type-Options**: Setting the **X-Content-Type-Options** header to `nosniff` instructs browsers not to override the detected MIME type of a resource, which can help prevent certain types of attacks such as MIME-sniffing attacks.

- **X-Frame-Options**: Setting the **X-Frame-Options** header to `DENY` or `SAMEORIGIN` can help prevent clickjacking attacks by specifying whether a browser should be allowed to render a page in a frame or iframe.

- **X-XSS-Protection**: Enabling the **X-XSS-Protection** header with a value of `1; mode=block` instructs browsers to enable their built-in XSS protection mechanisms, which can help detect and mitigate XSS attacks.

- **HTTP Strict Transport Security (HSTS)**: HSTS instructs browsers to only access a website over HTTPS, which helps prevent man-in-the-middle attacks and protocol downgrade attacks.

- **Referrer-Policy**: Setting the **Referrer-Policy** header to `strict-origin-when-cross-origin` or `same-origin` can help prevent information leakage by controlling how much referrer information is included in requests.

- **Cross-Origin Resource Sharing (CORS)**: Properly configuring CORS headers can help prevent unauthorized cross-origin requests, which can help mitigate certain injection attacks such as **Cross-Site Request Forgery (CSRF)**.

- **Feature Policy**: Feature Policy allows you to selectively enable, disable, or restrict browser features and APIs, which can help mitigate various attacks and vulnerabilities.

- **HTTP Public Key Pinning (HPKP)**: While HPKP has been deprecated due to potential risks, it was used to prevent certain attacks such as SSL/TLS certificate misissuance.

- **Incident response plan**: Developing an incident response plan for injection attacks is essential for effectively mitigating and responding to security incidents.

Awareness and education about secure coding practices are crucial to building robust web applications resistant to injection attacks.

Broken authentication and session management

Broken authentication and session management are security vulnerabilities that can lead to unauthorized access, identity theft, and other security breaches in software applications. These vulnerabilities arise when developers fail to implement proper authentication and session management mechanisms. One well-known example of a broken authentication attack is the Equifax data breach of 2017. Equifax, one of the largest credit reporting agencies in the United States, suffered a massive data breach that exposed sensitive personal information of approximately 147 million consumers.

Here's an overview of each:

- **Broken authentication**: Broken authentication occurs when attackers exploit flaws in the authentication process to gain unauthorized access to user accounts.

  - Common issues:

    - **Weak password policies**: A lack of password complexity requirements and enforcement of strong password policies

    - **Credential stuffing**: Attackers use leaked username-password pairs from one service to gain unauthorized access to another where users have reused credentials

    - **Insecure session management**: Poorly managed user sessions, such as session fixation or session hijacking

- **Session management**: Session management involves the secure creation, maintenance, and termination of user sessions after authentication.

  - Common issues:

    - **Session fixation**: Attackers set or hijack a user's session ID to gain unauthorized access to the victim's account

    - **Session timeout**: A lack of proper session timeout policies leads to sessions remaining active for an extended period, increasing the risk of unauthorized access

    - **Session invalidation**: An inability to invalidate or destroy sessions properly allows attackers to reuse or hijack inactive sessions

Preventive measures:

- **Secure authentication**:

  - Enforce strong password policies

  - Implement **Multi-Factor Authentication (MFA)** for an additional layer of security

  - Protect against credential stuffing attacks by monitoring and blocking suspicious login attempts

  - Protect against brute force and DoS attacks utilizing challenges

  - Implement secure lockout and account recovery policies

- **Secure session management**:

  - Use secure session management practices, including session encryption message encryption, and secure cookie attributes

  - Implement session timeout to log out inactive users automatically

  - Generate random and unique session identifiers to prevent session fixation attacks

  - Invalidate or regenerate session IDs upon login or privilege changes

- **Token-based authentication**:

  - For enhanced security, consider using token-based authentication mechanisms such as **JSON Web Tokens (JWTs)**

- **Regular security audits and standard compliance**:

  - Conduct regular security audits and penetration testing to identify and address vulnerabilities

  - Test for session management issues, such as session fixation and session hijacking

  - Ensure you comply with security standards such as PCI DSS

- **Education and training**:

  - Provide education and training for developers to raise awareness of secure authentication and session management practices

By addressing these issues and implementing best practices, developers can significantly reduce the risk of broken authentication and session management vulnerabilities in their software applications. Regularly updating and monitoring security measures is essential to stay ahead of evolving security threats.

Request forgery

Cross-Site Request Forgery (**CSRF**), is a web security vulnerability that occurs when an attacker fools the browser into doing an unwanted action on a third-party trusted site. The user is authenticated on the third-party site, and the CSRF attack exploits that authentication. One of the most infamous CSRF attacks occurred in 2008 and targeted the WordPress blogging application. The attack is known as the "Samy Worm" because Samy Kamkar created it.

Here's an overview of CSRF and preventive measures:

- **CSRF attack scenario**:

  - An attacker tricks a user into loading a page that contains a malicious request

  - The malicious request is crafted to act on a target site where the user is authenticated (e.g., changing account settings or making a purchase)

- Since the user is authenticated on the target site, the browser includes the user's session cookie in the request, making it appear legitimate to the target site

- The target site unknowingly processes the malicious request, leading to unintended actions

- **Preventive measures against CSRF:**

  - **Anti-CSRF tokens:** Include anti-CSRF tokens in forms and requests. These tokens are unique to each user session and are required to validate the legitimacy of a request. Without the correct token, the request is rejected.

  - **SameSite Cookie Attribute:** Set the `SameSite` attribute on cookies to control when they are sent with cross-site requests. Setting it to **Strict** or **Lax** can help mitigate CSRF attacks.

  - **Referer header checking:** Check the **Referer** header on incoming requests to ensure they originate from the same domain. However, relying solely on the **Referer** header is not foolproof, as it can sometimes be manipulated or stripped.

  - **Custom headers:** Include custom headers in requests expected to be present only for legitimate requests initiated by the application.

  - **Double-submit cookies:** Ensure that the anti-CSRF token is stored in both a cookie and as a request parameter. The server can then compare the values to verify the request's legitimacy.

  - **Content-type validation:** Verify that requests have the correct **Content-Type** header to prevent specific CSRF attacks that rely on image tags or other content types to trigger actions.

Figure 9.1 illustrates the prevention of CSRF attacks through CSRF tokens. Here's a breakdown of the components:

- **Authentication:** Represents the authentication module responsible for user authentication

- **Controller:** Represents the application controller responsible for handling requests

- **View:** Represents the view responsible for rendering the web page

- **Browser:** Represents the user's browser, where the CSRF token is generated and included in requests

- **Server:** Represents the server handling the incoming requests and validating CSRF tokens

- **Database:** Represents the database where the server processes the requests

The `<<CSRFToken.generate()>>` stereotype indicates that a CSRF token is generated and included in the request made by the browser. The server then validates the CSRF token to ensure the authenticity of the request.

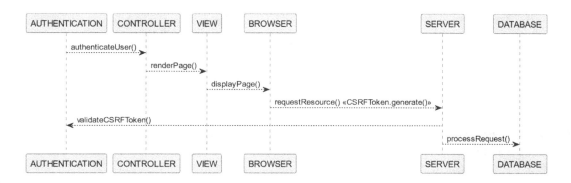

Figure 9.1 – UML sequence diagram showing CSRF tokens

- Here are some implementation best practices:

  - **Secure coding practices**: Follow secure coding practices to avoid introducing vulnerabilities that CSRF attacks could exploit

  - **Session management**: Implement secure session management practices, including session timeout and secure session token generation

  - **Security audits**: Regularly conduct security audits and testing, including penetration testing, to identify and address potential CSRF vulnerabilities

By incorporating these preventive measures into web application development, developers can significantly reduce the risk of CSRF attacks and enhance the overall security of their applications. It's crucial to stay informed about emerging security threats and keep security mechanisms current.

Language-specific defenses

Defending against standard web attacks requires implementing security measures specific to the programming language used in a web application. Here are some language-specific defenses against common web attacks:

- **PHP**:

  - **Filter input data**: Use functions such as `filter_input()` or `mysqli_real_escape_string()` to sanitize user input and prevent SQL injection

  - **Prepared statements**: Employ prepared statements and parameterized queries to protect against SQL injection attacks

  - **Cross-Site Scripting (XSS) prevention**: Use `htmlspecialchars()` or `htmlentities()` to escape user input when displaying it in HTML to prevent XSS attacks

  - **Session security**: Store session data securely, use secure session handling functions, and regenerate session IDs after successful logins.

- **Content Security Policy (CSP)**: Implement CSP headers to control which resources can be loaded and mitigate XSS attacks.

- Java:

  - **Input validation**: Validate and sanitize user input to prevent common vulnerabilities such as SQL injection and XSS

  - **Hibernate ORM**: If using Hibernate for database interactions, leverage features such as parameterized queries to prevent SQL injection

  - **Anti-CSRF tokens**: Implement anti-CSRF tokens to protect against CSRF attacks

  - **Security headers**: Utilize security headers, including **Strict-Transport-Security (HSTS)**, **Content-Security-Policy (CSP)**, and X-Content-Type-Options, to enhance web security.

- **Python (Django/Flask)**:

  - **Django (Python framework)**:

    - **Django ORM**: Leverage the Django ORM's protection against SQL injection attacks.

    - **Cross-Site Scripting (XSS) prevention**: Django templates automatically escape variables, providing protection against XSS.

    - **CSRF protection**: Django includes built-in CSRF protection. Ensure it's enabled.

  - **Flask (Python microframework)**:

    - **SQLAlchemy ORM**: Use SQLAlchemy with Flask to prevent SQL injection

    - **Secure cookies**: Enable secure session cookies in Flask for improved session security

    - **Security headers**: Set security headers to enhance overall web security

- **Node.js (JavaScript)**:

  - **Input validation**: Use libraries such as `validator` and `express-validator` to validate and sanitize user input

  - **NoSQL injection prevention**: If using NoSQL databases, parameterize queries to prevent injection attacks

  - **Helmet middleware**: Use the `helmet` middleware to set various HTTP headers for enhanced security, including XSS and CSRF protection

  - **Session security**: Implement secure session management using libraries such as `express-session`

- **Ruby (Ruby on Rails)**:

  - **Active Record ORM**: Leverage the features of the Active Record ORM to protect against SQL injection.

  - **Cross-Site Scripting (XSS) prevention**: Utilize built-in helpers such as h() to escape user input in views.

  - **CSRF protection**: Ruby on Rails includes built-in CSRF protection. Ensure it's enabled in the application.

  - **Content Security Policy (CSP)**: Implement CSP headers to mitigate XSS attacks.

These are general guidelines; staying updated with the latest security best practices for each programming language and its associated frameworks is crucial. Regular security audits, code reviews, and testing are essential to maintain a secure web application. Also, ensure that your tooling is updated and that you store changes to your source code in version control.

Example of enterprise web defenses

Throughout this book, we will build a secure design for an event ticketing system. Envision a software system that allows a box office or a website to sell tickets to a famous musical concert or theatre event. In the previous chapter, we covered code that will properly validate and sanitize input, which is the best defense against XSS. The next chapter will look at code to defend against SQL injection.

To defend against CSRF attacks in PHP, you can use anti-CSRF tokens. Here's a simple example of how to implement CSRF protection using tokens:

- Generate a CSRF token on the server side and include it in the form.

- Verify the token when processing the form submission.

Here's the example PHP code:

```php
<?php
session_start();
session_regenerate_id();

function generateCSRFToken() {
    $token = bin2hex(random_bytes(32)); // Generate a random token
    $_SESSION['csrf_token'] = $token; // Store it in the session
    return $token;
}

function validateCSRFToken($token) {
    return isset($_SESSION['csrf_token']) && hash_equals($_
SESSION['csrf_token'], $token);
```

```
}

// Generate token when rendering the form
$csrfToken = generateCSRFToken();
?>

<!DOCTYPE html>
<html lang="en">
<head>
    <meta charset="UTF-8">
    <meta name="viewport" content="width=device-width, initial-
      scale=1.0">
    <title>CSRF Protected Form</title>
</head>
<body>

<form action="process_form.php" method="post">
    <!-- Include the CSRF token in the form -->
    <input type="hidden" name="csrf_token" value="<?php echo
      $csrfToken; ?>">

    <!-- Your other form fields go here -->

    <button type="submit">Submit</button>
</form>

</body>
</html>
```

In the process_form.php file that is located on the server processed when the above client HTML form is submitted:

```
<?php
session_start();

// Validate CSRF token before processing the form data
if ($_SERVER['REQUEST_METHOD'] === 'POST' && validateCSRFToken($_
POST['csrf_token'])) {
    // Process the form data
    // ...

    // After processing, regenerate a new CSRF token for the next form
    //submission
    $newCSRFToken = generateCSRFToken();
```

```
} else {
    // CSRF token validation failed
    // Handle the error or redirect as needed
}
?>
```

This example uses the `random_bytes` function to generate a random token and the `hash_equals` function to compare the stored token with the one submitted in the form. Additionally, the token is regenerated after each successful form submission to mitigate the risk of token reuse. The code requires PHP7 or greater for the `random_bytes` function. It is important to ensure your PHP environment has a supported version with all the latest patches.

We also want to have secure session management in our enterprise ticketing management. Secure session management is crucial for the security of web applications. Here are some best practices for secure session management in PHP:

- **Use session cookies securely**: Set the `session.cookie_secure` option to true in your PHP configuration to ensure that cookies are only sent over HTTPS. Set the `session.cookie_httponly` option to true to prevent JavaScript from accessing the session cookie:

  ```
  ini_set('session.cookie_secure', true);
  ini_set('session.cookie_httponly', true);
  ```

- **Use a strong session ID generator**: PHP uses a random number generator by default, but you can enhance it by setting `session.entropy_length` and `session.entropy_file`. Ensure that these values are configured appropriately for your environment:

  ```
  ini_set('session.entropy_length', 32);
  ini_set('session.entropy_file', '/dev/urandom');
  ```

- **Regenerate session ID**: Regenerate the session ID periodically to mitigate session fixation attacks. Use `session_regenerate_id()`:

  ```
  session_regenerate_id(true);
  ```

- **Set session timeout**: Set a reasonable session timeout to expire sessions automatically after a certain period of inactivity:

  ```
  ini_set('session.gc_maxlifetime', 1800); // 30 minutes
  ```

- **Store sessions securely**: Choose a secure session storage mechanism. PHP sessions can be stored in files, databases, or custom handlers. Ensure proper access controls for the session storage directory:

  ```
  // Example using a custom session save path
  session_save_path('/path/to/secure/session/directory');
  ```

- **Use session hashing**: If you store sessions in a database, hash the session data to add an extra layer of security.

- **Implement session expiry**: Implement your session expiry mechanism to ensure that sessions are correctly cleaned up when they expire.

- **Handle session data carefully**: Avoid storing sensitive information directly in the session. If necessary, encrypt sensitive data before storing it.

- **Regularly review and audit**: Review and audit your session management implementation for security vulnerabilities.

By following these best practices, you can enhance the security of session management in your PHP applications and reduce the risk of session-related attacks. Remember that security is an ongoing process; staying informed about the latest best practices and vulnerabilities is essential.

Summary

This chapter introduced standard web application vulnerabilities. We started by looking at injection attacks. Next, we looked at broken authentication and session management. We then discussed request forgery attacks. To defend against the standard attacks discussed, we explored programming language-specific defenses.

In the next chapter, we will drill into database security and look at defenses against SQL injection.

Self-assessment questions

1. What is **Cross-Site Scripting (XSS)**, and why is it a security concern for web applications?

    A. XSS is a security feature that prevents data leakage in web applications.

    B. XSS is a programming language used for web development.

    C. XSS is a technique used to secure web applications.

    D. XSS is a vulnerability that allows attackers to inject malicious scripts into web pages viewed by other users.

2. What is **Cross-Site Request Forgery (CSRF)** and how can web applications defend against it?

    A. CSRF is a technique for securely transmitting data between a client and a server.

    B. CSRF is a security feature that protects against unauthorized data access.

    C. CSRF is a type of encryption used to protect sensitive data in web applications.

    D. CSRF is an attack where an attacker tricks a user into unknowingly making a request to a web application without their consent.

3. What is SQL injection and how can it be prevented in web applications?

    A. SQL injection is a database management technique used to improve query performance.

    B. SQL injection is a security vulnerability that allows attackers to execute arbitrary SQL queries through user inputs.

    C. SQL injection is a feature in SQL databases used for optimizing data retrieval.

    D. SQL injection is a web application firewall used to block SQL requests.

4. What is the primary purpose of **Cross-Site Scripting (XSS)** attacks?

    A. Brute-force password attacks

    B. Stealing session cookies

    C. Exploiting server misconfigurations

    D. Executing malicious scripts on a user's browser

5. Which security mechanism helps protect against **Cross-Site Request Forgery (CSRF)** attacks?

    A. Content Security Policy (CSP)

    B. Two-Factor Authentication (2FA)

    C. Cross-Origin Resource Sharing (CORS)

    D. Anti-CSRF tokens

Answers

1. D

2. D

3. B

4. D

5. D

10

Database Security

Database security means implementing measures to protect the confidentiality, integrity, and availability of data stored in a database system. As databases often contain sensitive and valuable information, securing them is critical to prevent data breaches, unauthorized access, and data manipulation.

In this chapter, we're going to cover database security by looking at the following main topics:

- Overview of SQL
- SQL injection
- Correctness
- Concurrency
- Language-specific defenses
- RBAC security in DBMS
- Encryption in DBMS
- An example of enterprise DB security

By the end of this chapter, you will have a strong understanding of how SQL vulnerabilities can be reduced.

Overview of SQL

Structured Query Language (**SQL**) is a programming language for managing and manipulating relational databases. Here's an overview of crucial SQL concepts:

- **Database**: A collection of organized data. It can contain multiple tables, views, stored procedures, and more.
- **Table**: A structured set of data elements organized in rows and columns. Each column represents a different attribute, and each row is a record.

- **Column**: Represents a single data item in a table. It defines the type of data that can be stored in that column.

- **Row**: A record in a table containing data for each column defined in the table.

- **Primary key**: A unique identifier for each record in a table. It ensures that each row can be uniquely identified.

- **Foreign key**: A field in a database table that links to the primary key in another table. It establishes a link between the two tables.

- **Index**: A data structure that improves the speed of data retrieval operations on a database table.

- **Query**: A request for data or information from a database. SQL queries retrieve, update, insert, or delete data. The following are the major components of queries. The values in brackets should be replaced with actual column names, table names, or values:

- **SELECT statement**: Used to retrieve data from one or more tables. It is the most-used SQL command:

```
SELECT [column1], [column2] FROM [table] WHERE [condition];
```

- **INSERT statement**: Adds new records to a table with the values specified:

```
INSERT INTO [table] (column1, column2) VALUES ([value1],
[value2]);
```

- **UPDATE statement**: Modifies existing records in a table that passes the condition:

```
UPDATE [table] SET [column] = [value] WHERE [condition];
```

- **DELETE statement**: Removes records from a table:

```
DELETE FROM [table WHERE condition;
```

- **JOIN clause**: Combines rows from two or more tables based on a related column between them:

```
SELECT * FROM [table1] JOIN [table2] ON [table1.column] =
[table2.column];
```

- **WHERE clause**: Filters records based on a specified condition:

```
SELECT * FROM [table] WHERE [condition];
```

- **GROUP BY clause**: Groups rows with the same values into summary rows:

```
SELECT [column], COUNT(*) FROM [table] GROUP BY [column];
```

- **ORDER BY clause**: Sorts the result set in ascending or descending order:

```
SELECT * FROM [table] ORDER BY [column] ASC;
```

These are fundamental concepts; there is much more to SQL, including subqueries, stored procedures, triggers, and transactions. SQL is widely used in database management systems such as MySQL, PostgreSQL, SQLite, Microsoft SQL Server, and Oracle Database.

SQL injection

SQL injection is a cyberattack that occurs when an attacker inserts malicious SQL code into a query. This can happen when user input is not validated correctly or sanitized before being used in a SQL query. The goal of SQL injection is to manipulate the query in a way that allows unauthorized access to a database, retrieval of sensitive information, or modification of data.

Here are some critical points about SQL injection:

- **Vulnerable input points**: SQL injection typically occurs in web applications where user inputs, such as form fields or URL parameters, are directly incorporated into SQL queries without proper validation or parameterization. We discussed this in *Chapter 8* when we discussed input validation and sanitization.

- **Attack scenarios**:

  - Unauthorized access: Attackers may use SQL injection to bypass authentication mechanisms and gain unauthorized access to a system

  - Data retrieval: Attackers can manipulate queries to retrieve sensitive data from a database

  - Data modification: SQL injection can be used to modify or delete data in a database

- Example of SQL injection:

  Consider a login form with the following SQL query to check user credentials:

  ```
  SELECT * FROM users WHERE username = 'input_username' AND
  password = 'input_password';
  ```

  An attacker might input the following in the username field:

  ```
  ' OR '1'='1'; --
  ```

  The modified query becomes:

  ```
  SELECT * FROM users WHERE username = '' OR '1'='1'; --' AND
  password = 'input_password';
  ```

  The double hyphen (- -) comments out the remaining part of the original query, allowing the attacker to log in without a valid password.

- Prevention techniques:

  - Parameterized statements: Use parameterized queries or prepared statements, where user input is treated as a parameter rather than directly embedded in the SQL query

- Input validation: Validate and sanitize user input to ensure it meets expected patterns and doesn't contain malicious code

- Least-privilege principle: Ensure that database accounts used by web applications have the minimum necessary permissions

- Security best practices:

  - Regularly update and patch your web application and database software.

  - Employ a **web application firewall** (**WAF**) to detect and prevent SQL injection attacks. We discussed this in *Chapter 9* when we discussed standard web application attacks.

  - Conduct security audits and penetration testing to identify and address vulnerabilities.

Understanding and implementing proper security measures is crucial to prevent SQL injection and protect sensitive data in applications.

Maintaining database correctness

Ensuring database correctness is crucial for maintaining data integrity, accuracy, and reliability. Here are some key aspects of and best practices to achieve and maintain database correctness:

- Data validation:

  - Enforce data validation rules at the database level to ensure that only valid and expected data is stored

  - Use constraints (e.g., NOT NULL, unique constraints) to prevent incorrect or incomplete data insertion

- Data accuracy:

  - Regularly perform data quality checks and validation to identify and correct inaccuracies.

  - Implement mechanisms to validate data accuracy during data entry and update processes. We covered this some in *Chapter 8* when we discussed input validation and sanitization.

- Referential integrity:

  - Use foreign key constraints to maintain referential integrity between related tables

  - Ensure relationships between tables are well defined and data dependencies are maintained

- Normalization:

  - Apply normalization techniques to organize data efficiently and reduce redundancy

  - Normalize tables to minimize data update anomalies and improve overall data consistency

- **Atomicity, Consistency, Isolation, Durability (ACID):**
  - Follow ACID principles to ensure transactions are processed reliably
  - Transactions should be atomic (indivisible), consistent (maintain data integrity), isolated (not affected by other transactions), and durable (persist even in the event of a system failure)

- Concurrency control:
  - Implement mechanisms to control concurrent access to the database to prevent data inconsistencies
  - Use locking, isolation levels, and optimistic or pessimistic concurrency control

- Data auditing and logging:
  - Enable auditing features to track changes to the database, including inserts, updates, and deletes
  - Maintain comprehensive logs for monitoring and troubleshooting purposes

- Backup and recovery:
  - Regularly perform database backups to safeguard against data loss
  - Implement a robust disaster recovery plan to ensure quick and reliable recovery in the event of data corruption or system failure

- Data versioning:
  - Implement versioning for critical data to track changes over time
  - This is particularly useful for historical analysis and auditing purposes
  - This can be done within the table by storing the version number, but some database systems store all versions and never actually delete data

- Testing and validation:
  - Conduct thorough testing of database operations, including input validation, queries, and transactions
  - Perform regular data validation checks and conduct periodic audits

- Security measures:
  - Implement strong access controls and authentication mechanisms to prevent unauthorized access
  - Regularly review and update security policies and practices

- Documentation:

  - Maintain comprehensive documentation of the database schema, relationships, and data validation rules

  - Document procedures for data maintenance, updates, and schema changes

By adhering to these best practices and principles, you can help ensure the correctness of your database, which is crucial for maintaining the reliability and trustworthiness of your data-driven applications. Regular monitoring, testing, and proactive measures contribute to a robust database environment.

Managing activity concurrency

Concurrency in databases refers to the ability of a **database management system (DBMS)** to handle multiple transactions or operations simultaneously without compromising data integrity. Concurrency control mechanisms are essential to ensure that multiple users or processes can access and manipulate data concurrently without causing conflicts or inconsistencies. Here are key concepts related to database concurrency:

- Isolation levels:

  - Isolation levels define the degree to which the operations of one transaction are isolated from the operations of other concurrent transactions.

  - Common isolation levels include READ UNCOMMITTED, READ COMMITTED, REPEATABLE READ, and SERIALIZABLE. You can think of these isolation levels as a trade-off between increased availability and lower consistency. This is because locks are used to ensure the separation of transactions in stronger isolation levels, leading to lower concurrency levels.

- Locking:

  - Locks are mechanisms used to control access to data during transactions to prevent conflicts

  - Types of locks:

    - Shared locks: Allow multiple transactions to read a resource simultaneously but prevent any of them from writing to it

    - Exclusive locks: Prevent other transactions from acquiring any lock (shared or exclusive) on a resource

- Concurrency control techniques:

  - **Optimistic Concurrency Control (OCC):**

    - Assumes that conflicts between transactions are rare

    - Allows transactions to proceed without locks and checks for conflicts only at the end

- If conflicts are detected, the system rolls back one or more transactions

  - Pessimistic concurrency control:

    - Relies on locks to prevent conflicts between transactions

    - May use shared or exclusive locks based on the operations being performed

- Timestamp ordering:

  - Assigns a unique timestamp to each transaction

  - Transactions are ordered based on their timestamps, and conflicts are resolved accordingly

- **Multi-Version Concurrency Control (MVCC):**

  - Allows multiple versions of a data item to coexist in the database

  - Each transaction sees a snapshot of the data as it existed at the start of the transaction

- Deadlocks:

  - A deadlock occurs when two or more transactions are blocked, each waiting for the other to release a lock

  - DBMSs typically have mechanisms to detect and resolve deadlocks, such as timeout and deadlock detection algorithms

- Conflict resolution:

  - When conflicts arise, the DBMS needs mechanisms to resolve them, either by rolling back transactions, delaying transactions, or using other strategies

- Read and write operations:

  - Different concurrency control strategies may be employed for read and write operations

  - Read operations may use less restrictive locks or no locks at all, while write operations typically require exclusive locks

- Consistency and integrity:

  - Concurrency control mechanisms aim to maintain the consistency and integrity of the database despite concurrent access

- Application design:

  - Well-designed applications should consider concurrency control from the beginning

  - Use transactions effectively and minimize the time that transactions hold locks for

- Monitoring and tuning:

  - Regularly monitor the database for performance and concurrency issues

  - Tune the concurrency control mechanisms based on the workload and requirements

Database concurrency is a complex topic, and the choice of concurrency control mechanisms depends on factors such as the application's requirements, the nature of the data, and performance considerations. Properly managing concurrency ensures that databases can handle concurrent access while maintaining data integrity and consistency.

Language-specific defenses

Securing databases involves implementing specific measures to protect against potential vulnerabilities and attacks. Here are language-specific defenses for programming languages commonly used in web development:

- SQL:

  - Parameterized statements/prepared statements:

    - Use parameterized queries or prepared statements to separate SQL code from user input

    - This prevents SQL injection attacks by ensuring that user input is treated as data rather than executable code

  - Stored procedures:

    - Utilize stored procedures to encapsulate and execute SQL logic on the database server

    - This can limit the exposure of SQL code to potential attackers

- PHP:

  - **PHP Data Objects (PDO):**

    - Prefer using PDO over older MySQL functions

    - PDO supports parameterized queries, reducing the risk of SQL injection

  - MySQLi extension:

    - If using MySQL, consider the MySQLi extension, which supports parameterized queries and provides improved security features

  - Escaping user input:

    - Use functions like `mysqli_real_escape_string` to escape user input before incorporating it into SQL queries

- Python (Django and Flask):

  - **Object-Relational Mapping (ORMs):**

    - Utilize ORM frameworks such as Django ORM (for Django) or SQLAlchemy (for Flask) to interact with databases

    - ORM frameworks often provide built-in protections against SQL injection by abstracting SQL queries

  - Query parameterization:

    - Using parameterized queries to mitigate SQL injection risks when writing raw SQL queries

  - Input validation:

    - Implement proper input validation to ensure data conforms to expected patterns before interacting with the database

- Java (Spring):

  - **Java Persistence API (JPA):**

    - Use JPA, a Java specification for managing relational data, to interact with databases

    - JPA implementations such as the Hibernate protect against SQL injection

  - `PreparedStatement` interface:

    - When using **Java Database Connectivity (JDBC)**, prefer `PreparedStatement` over `Statement` to handle parameterized queries

  - Input validation:

    - Validate user input to ensure it meets expected patterns and constraints before using it in database operations

- Node.js (Express):

  - ORMs (Sequelize, TypeORM):

    - Employ ORM libraries such as Sequelize or TypeORM to interact with databases

- ORM libraries often provide protection against SQL injection.

  - Parameterized queries:

    - Use parameterized queries when interacting with databases using raw SQL

- Input validation:

  - Implement input validation to sanitize and validate user inputs before using them in database operations

- C# (.NET):

  - Entity Framework:

    - Utilize Entity Framework for database interactions in .NET applications

    - Entity Framework includes mechanisms to prevent SQL injection

  - The `SqlParameter` class:

    - When working with raw SQL queries, use `SqlParameter` to parameterize queries and avoid SQL injection vulnerabilities

  - Input validation:

    - Implement proper input validation to ensure data integrity and security

Regardless of the programming language, it's essential to stay informed about security best practices, regularly update dependencies, and conduct security audits to identify and address potential vulnerabilities in database interactions.

RBAC security in DBMS

Role-Based Access Control (RBAC) is a widely used access control mechanism in database systems. RBAC provides a flexible and scalable approach to managing access permissions by associating users with roles and defining the privileges associated with each role. We introduced access control back in *Chapter 7* when we discussed authentication and authorization. Let's explore RBAC in the context of database systems.

The key concepts of RBAC in database systems are the following:

- **Roles**:

  - Definition: Roles represent a set of permissions or privileges

  - Purpose: Users are assigned roles, each with specific access rights

  - Example: Roles can be defined for different job functions such as "Admin," "Manager," or "Employee"

- **Users**:

  - Definition: Users are individuals or entities granted access to the database

- Association: Users are assigned to one or more roles based on their responsibilities

- Example: A user with the "Manager" role may have more privileges than one with the "Employee" role

- **Privileges**:

  - Definition: Privileges define the actions or operations that users in a role can perform

  - Granularity: RBAC allows fine-grained control over privileges, specifying what operations are allowed on specific database objects

  - Example: Privileges may include SELECT, INSERT, UPDATE, DELETE on tables, or EXECUTE on stored procedures

- **Role hierarchy**:

  - Definition: Roles can be organized into a hierarchy, where higher-level roles inherit the permissions of lower-level roles

  - Purpose: Simplifies management by allowing the assignment of a single higher-level role rather than multiple lower-level roles

  - Example: A "Supervisor" role may inherit permissions from both "Manager" and "Employee" roles

- **Dynamic assignment**:

  - Definition: Users can be dynamically assigned to roles based on their current responsibilities or context

  - Purpose: Enables dynamic adaptation of access rights as users' roles change

  - Example: Temporary user assignment to a "Project Team" role for the duration of a specific project

- **Policy administration**:

  - Definition: RBAC policies are defined and administered by database administrators

  - Centralized control: Policies are centrally managed, making enforcing consistent access controls across the database easier

  - Example: An administrator may create, modify, or delete roles and their associated privileges

The benefits of using RBAC in database systems include the following:

- Simplified administration: RBAC simplifies the administration of access controls by grouping users into roles

- Scalability: As the number of users and permissions grows, RBAC provides a scalable solution for managing access

- Flexibility: RBAC allows for flexible assignment of roles and dynamic adaptation of access rights

- Reduced Errors: Centralized control and role-based assignments reduce the likelihood of errors in managing access permissions

- Security: RBAC enhances security by ensuring that users only have the necessary permissions for their roles, limiting the potential impact of security breaches

Implementing RBAC in a database system contributes to efficient access management, enhanced security, and simplified administration, making it a valuable component of a comprehensive database security strategy.

Encryption in DBMS

Encryption in databases is a critical aspect of database security, aimed at protecting sensitive data from unauthorized access or disclosure. Encryption involves transforming data into a secure, unreadable format using cryptographic algorithms. Here are the key aspects of encryption in databases:

- Types of database encryption:

  - Data-at-rest encryption:

    - Purpose: Encrypts data when stored on disk or other storage media

    - Protection: Guards against unauthorized access to the physical storage medium (e.g., hard drives or SSDs)

  - Data-in-transit encryption:

    - Purpose: Secures data as it is transmitted between the database server and clients

    - Protection: Safeguards against interception and eavesdropping during data transmission over networks

  - Data-in-use encryption:

    - Purpose: Focuses on protecting data while it is being processed or used by applications

    - Protection: Guards against unauthorized access during computations or processing stages

- Encryption algorithms:

  - Symmetric encryption: Uses a single key for both encryption and decryption. Fast and efficient but requires secure key management.

  - Asymmetric encryption: Involves a pair of public and private keys. The public key is used for encryption and the private key for decryption. Commonly used for secure key exchange.

- Hash functions: Used for creating digital signatures and ensuring data integrity. Hash functions are one-way functions, making it computationally infeasible to reverse the process.

- Database encryption methods:

  - **Transparent Data Encryption (TDE):**

    - Implementation: Encrypts the entire database, making it transparent to applications and users

    - Advantages: Simplifies implementation and doesn't require application changes

  - Column-level encryption:

    - Implementation: Encrypts specific columns containing sensitive information

    - Advantages: Granular control over encrypted data allows selective sensitivity-based encryption

  - Application-layer encryption:

    - Implementation: Encryption is handled by the application before storing or after retrieving data from the database

    - Advantages: Gives the application complete control over encryption logic and key management

- Key management:

  - Key generation: Secure generation and management of encryption keys are crucial. Keys should be random, complex, and securely stored.

  - Key rotation: Regularly changing encryption keys enhances security and mitigates risks associated with long-term key exposure.

  - Secure key storage: Protecting encryption keys from unauthorized access is vital. **Hardware Security Modules (HSMs)** provide secure key storage.

- Challenges and considerations:

  - Performance impact: Encryption may introduce some performance overhead, and careful consideration is needed to balance security and performance.

  - Data recovery: Adequate mechanisms for data recovery in case of key loss or system failure should be in place.

  - Regulatory compliance: Encryption is often required to comply with data protection regulations. A good example here is with storing credit card numbers to meet the PCI DSS standard the data must be encrypted.

The benefits of database encryption are as follows:

- Confidentiality: Encryption protects sensitive data from unauthorized access, ensuring confidentiality

- Integrity: it prevents unauthorized modifications to data by ensuring that only authorized parties can decrypt and modify information

- Compliance: It helps meet regulatory requirements for data protection and privacy

- Data-in-transit security: It safeguards data during transmission over networks

- Mitigation of insider threats: Encryption limits the risk of internal users accessing sensitive data without proper authorization

A robust encryption strategy is essential to overall database security, providing a solid defense against unauthorized access and data breaches.

An example of enterprise DB security

Throughout this book, we are building a secure design for an event ticketing system. Envision a software system that allows a box office or a website to sell tickets for a famous musical concert or theatre event. In this section, we will focus on utilizing prepared statements. The following code will create a simple events table in a MySQL database from PHP code. It will then prepare an INSERT statement with two parameters: an integer and a string. The bind_param creates the link between the variables and the parameters. The execute statement will do the actual insert:

```php
<?php

mysqli_report(MYSQLI_REPORT_ERROR | MYSQLI_REPORT_STRICT);
$mysqli = new mysqli("example.com", "user", "password", "database");

/* Non-prepared statement */
$mysqli->query("DROP TABLE IF EXISTS event");
$mysqli->query("CREATE TABLE event(id INT, Name varchar(255))");

/* Prepared statement, stage 1: prepare */
$stmt = $mysqli->prepare("INSERT INTO event(id, name) VALUES (?, ?)");
/* Prepared statement, stage 2: bind and execute */
$id = 1;
$name = 'Mean Girls';
$stmt->bind_param("is", $id, $name); // "is" means that $id is bound
as an integer and $name as a string

$stmt->execute();
?>
```

In a real application, the data will come from a web form. The following code demonstrates this concept and table with an input form in HTML and the backend PHP page that uses the prepared statement to insert the value:

```
<form action="saveevent.php">
    <label for="id">Id:</label>
    <input name="id" id="id"><br>
    <label for="name" >Name:</label>
    <input name="name" id="name"><br>
    <input type="submit" value"Submit:>
</form>
```

The action in the preceding form will send the values of the two input parameters to the following backend PHP code:

```
<?php
mysqli_report(MYSQLI_REPORT_ERROR | MYSQLI_REPORT_STRICT);
$mysqli = new mysqli("example.com", "user", "password", "database");

$stmt = $mysqli->prepare("INSERT INTO event(id, name) VALUES (?, ?)");
/* Prepared statement, stage 2: bind and execute */
$id = $_REQUEST["id"];
$name = $_REQUEST["name"];
$stmt->bind_param("is", $id, $name);
$stmt->execute();
?>
```

The code is similar to the earlier example but pulls the values from the $_REQUEST variable. This is the vulnerable code. The use of prepared statements to communicate with the database reduces the risk. The code here was kept simple to highlight the prepared statements but the input should also be sanitized as we discussed in previous chapters.

Summary

This chapter introduces the concepts behind database security. We started out by looking at how our applications communicate with databases via SQL. Next, we looked at attacks against this code. We followed this with several essential discussions around correctness and concurrency in databases. Correctness and proper concurrency structure help to protect the data from malicious users and natural issues. We looked at the tools available for different programming languages, how role-based security works in databases, and how we can use encryption to protect the confidentiality of our data. In the next chapter, we begin our journey into software testing and validation.

Self-assessment questions

1. What is the purpose of encryption in database security?

    A. Data compression

    B. Data obfuscation

    C. Data integrity

    D. Data confidentiality

2. What does SQL injection target in a database system?

    A. Application layer vulnerabilities

    B. Data integrity

    C. Authentication system

    D. Database schema

3. What is the purpose of **role-based access control** (**RBAC**) in database security?

    A. Encrypting data at rest

    B. Detecting and preventing SQL injection

    C. Filtering network traffic

    D. Controlling access based on user roles

4. Which database construct enforces correctness?

    A. Constraints

    B. Tables

    C. Stored Procedures

    D. Views

5. What tool in DBMSs helps with dynamic queries based on user input?

    A. Prepared statements

    B. Isolation levels

    C. Select statements

    D. Update statements

Answers

1. D
2. A
3. D
4. A
5. A

Part 3:
Security Validation

The third part of the book looks at ways to validate we delivered software that met both the functional and non-functional requirements specified earlier in the process.

This part has the following chapters:

11

Unit Testing

Unit testing is a software testing technique that involves testing individual units or components of a software application in isolation, ensuring that they work correctly. These units are typically minor testable software parts, such as functions, methods, or classes. The primary purpose of unit testing is to validate that each unit of code performs its intended functionality as expected.

In this chapter, we're going to cover unit testing by looking at the following main topics:

- The principles of unit testing
- The advantages of unit testing
- Unit testing frameworks
- An example of enterprise secure unit tests

By the end of the chapter, you will have learned the benefits of unit testing and how it can contribute to more secure and reliable software.

The principles of unit testing

Following certain principles helps create practical and maintainable unit tests. Here are some fundamental unit testing principles:

- **Isolation**: Each unit test should be isolated from other tests to ensure that the outcome of one test does not affect another. Isolation helps identify the cause of failures and makes tests more predictable.

- **Independence**: Unit tests should be independent of each other. The order in which tests are executed should not matter, and each test should produce consistent results regardless of the context in which it is run.

- **Fast fxecution**: Unit tests should be fast to execute. Fast execution encourages developers to run tests frequently, providing quick feedback on the code changes. Rapid tests are essential for incorporating testing into the development workflow.

- **Repeatable**: A unit test should produce the same results every time it is executed. A repeatable test ensures that failures can be consistently reproduced and investigated.

- **Focused**: Each unit test should test a specific behavior or functionality. Avoid trying multiple things in a single test, making it harder to identify the cause of a failure.

- **Clear and readable**: Write clear and readable tests so that developers can easily understand the purpose and expected behavior of the tested code. Use descriptive names for tests and follow a consistent testing style.

- **Maintainability**: Unit tests should be easy to maintain. If the code under test changes, the corresponding tests should be updated promptly to reflect those changes. Well-maintained tests contribute to the overall health and reliability of the code base.

- **Automation**: Unit tests should be automated to enable frequent and consistent execution. Automation helps ensure that tests are run whenever code changes are made, reducing the chances of introducing bugs.

- **Single responsibility**: Follow the single responsibility principle for tests as you do for your code. Each test should have a single reason to fail, making identifying and fixing issues easier.

- **Mocking and stubbing**: Use mocking and stubbing techniques to isolate the unit under test from external dependencies. Mocking and stubbing allow you to focus on testing the specific behavior of the unit without being affected by the behavior of its dependencies.

By adhering to these principles, developers can create effective, reliable, and maintainable unit tests, essential for building robust and high-quality software.

The advantages of unit testing

Unit testing offers several advantages that contribute to software's overall quality, reliability, and maintainability. Here are some key benefits of unit testing:

- **Early bug detection**: Unit tests enable the early detection of bugs and issues in code. Since unit tests are written alongside the code, developers can identify and fix problems as soon as they occur, reducing the likelihood of more complex and costly problems later in the development process.

- **Facilitating code refactoring**: Unit tests provide a safety net when refactoring code. Developers can confidently make changes to the code base, knowing that if any existing functionality is affected, the unit tests will catch it. Refactoring encourages code improvement and the implementation of design changes.

- **Documentation**: Unit tests serve as documentation for the code. By looking at the unit tests, developers can understand the intended behavior of the code, making it easier to work with and maintain.

- **Continuous integration support**: Unit tests are integral to continuous integration practices. Automated build processes can run unit tests whenever there are code changes, providing rapid feedback to developers about the impact of their changes on existing functionality.

- **Improved code quality**: Writing unit tests encourage developers to adopt good coding practices. It promotes modular and loosely coupled design, leading to more maintainable and understandable code. The act of testing often results in cleaner and more reliable code.

- **Regression testing**: Unit tests act as regression testing. When new features are added, or changes are made, running the existing suite of unit tests helps ensure that previously implemented functionality still works as intended.

- **Enhancing collaboration**: Unit tests are executable documentation to share among team members. They provide a common understanding of how different parts of a system are expected to behave, fostering collaboration among team members.

- **Cost savings**: Although writing unit tests requires an initial investment, it can save time and resources in the long run. Early bug detection and prevention of regression issues reduce the overall cost of development and maintenance.

- **Increasing confidence in code changes**: Developers gain confidence in making changes to the code base when there is a comprehensive suite of passing unit tests. This confidence is precious in large and complex projects where understanding the impact of changes can be challenging.

- **Easier debugging**: When a unit test fails, it clearly indicates which part of the code base does not function as expected. Unit tests make the debugging process more efficient, as developers can focus on the specific area of concern.

Leveraging these advantages makes unit testing a fundamental practice in software development, contributing to creating robust, maintainable, and high-quality software products.

Unit testing frameworks

Unit testing frameworks help developers create, organize, and run unit tests for their code. These frameworks provide a structure for writing tests, offer a set of assertions to check expected outcomes, and facilitate the automation of test execution. There are numerous unit test frameworks available for various programming languages. Here are some popular ones for different languages:

- **JUnit (Java)**: JUnit is a widely used unit testing framework for Java. It provides annotations to define test methods, fixtures for setup and teardown, and assertions to verify expected outcomes.

- **TestNG (Java)**: TestNG is another testing framework for Java that is inspired by JUnit but offers additional features, such as support for parallel test execution, flexible test configuration, and data-driven testing.

- **NUnit (.NET – C#, VB.NET, and F#)**: NUnit is a unit testing framework for .NET languages such as C#, VB.NET, and F#. It supports a range of test fixtures, assertions, and attributes to control the test execution flow.

- **xUnit.net (.NET – C# and F#)**: xUnit.net is a modern and extensible testing framework for .NET. It follows the xUnit principles and is designed to be more extensible and developer-friendly. It supports parallel test execution and features a clean and extensible architecture.

- **pytest (Python)**: `pytest` is a popular testing framework for Python. It provides a simple syntax for writing tests, supports fixtures for setup and teardown, and has extensive plugin support. pytest can be easily integrated with other testing tools.

- **unittest (Python)**: `unittest`, sometimes referred to as "PyUnit," is the built-in testing framework for Python. It is inspired by JUnit and follows a similar structure, offering test discovery, test fixtures, and assertion methods.

- **Mocha (JavaScript – Node.js and browser)**: Mocha is a versatile testing framework for JavaScript, commonly used for both Node.js and browser-based applications. It supports various assertion libraries asynchronous testing and has a flexible test structure.

- **Jest (JavaScript – Node.js and browser)**: Jest is a testing framework developed by Facebook for JavaScript, focusing on simplicity and speed. It includes features such as snapshot testing, mocking, and parallel test execution.

- **PHPUnit (PHP)**: PHPUnit is a unit-testing framework for PHP. It provides a range of testing functionality, including support for fixtures, data providers, and mocking. PHPUnit is widely used in PHP projects.

- **CppUTest (C++)**: CppUTest is a unit testing framework for C++ that follows a syntax similar to other xUnit frameworks. It is designed for embedded and desktop C++ projects, providing a lightweight, easy-to-use testing solution.

When choosing a unit test framework, consider factors such as community support, documentation, integration with other development tools, and ease of use based on your programming language and project requirements.

An example of enterprise threat model

Throughout this book, we will build a secure design for an event ticketing system. Envision a software system that allows a box office or a website to sell tickets to a famous musical concert or theatre event. We will demonstrate unit tests in three languages, PHP, Java, and Python, to test the `Person` class from our object model. This chapter will test a single method, but all methods with interesting behavior should have unit tests written. If you remember from our object, the `create_login` method takes in a password. We want to ensure the password has a length of eight characters or greater, uses both uppercase and lowercase characters, and has at least one symbol.

> **Note:**
>
> Naming conventions and consistency are important to improve software quality. We are using an example across many programming languages. In some languages, `create_login` should be written as `createLogin` to maintain language convention. You will see this later in the JUnit test examples.

PHPUnit

To write PHPUnit tests for a `Person` class with a `create_login` method that enforces password requirements, we first need to define the class:

```php
<?php

class Person
{
    private $first_name;
    private $last_name;
    private $email;
    private $password;

    public function __construct($email)
    {
        $this->email = $email;
    }

    public function create_login($password)
    {
        if ($this->isValidPassword($password)) {
            $this->password = $password;
            return true;
        } else {
            return false;
        }
    }

    private function isValidPassword($password)
    {
        return strlen($password) >= 8
            && preg_match('/[a-z]/', $password)
            && preg_match('/[A-Z]/', $password)
            && preg_match('/[!@#$%^&*()\-_=+{};:,<.>]/', $password);
    }
```

```php
    public function getPassword()
    {
        return $this->password;
    }
}
```

Next, we write PHPUnit tests for this `Person` class. You need to create a test class with methods to test various scenarios:

```php
<?php

use PHPUnit\Framework\TestCase;

class PersonTest extends TestCase
{
    public function testValidPassword()
    {
        $person = new Person('testUser@aol.com');
        $this->assertTrue($person->create_login('ValidPass1!'));
        $this->assertEquals('ValidPass1!', $person->getPassword());
    }

    public function testInvalidShortPassword()
    {
        $person = new Person('testUser@aol.com');
        $this->assertFalse($person->create_login('Short1!'));
        $this->assertNull($person->getPassword());
    }

    public function testInvalidNoLowerCasePassword()
    {
        $person = new Person('testUser@aol.com');
        $this->assertFalse($person->create_login('UPPERCASE1!'));
        $this->assertNull($person->getPassword());
    }

    public function testInvalidNoUpperCasePassword()
    {
        $person = new Person('testUser@aol.com');
        $this->assertFalse($person->create_login('lowercase1!'));
        $this->assertNull($person->getPassword());
    }

    public function testInvalidNoSymbolPassword()
```

```
    {
        $person = new Person('testUser@aol.com');
        $this->assertFalse($person->create_login('NoSymbol123'));
        $this->assertNull($person->getPassword());
    }
}
```

You can run these tests using PHPUnit. Make sure you have PHPUnit installed, and then run the following:

```
phpunit YourTestClassFileName.php
```

Let's break down the code:

- **Namespace and use statement**: This line includes the necessary PHPUnit framework classes to write test cases.

  ```
  use PHPUnit\Framework\TestCase;
  ```

- **Test class definition**: This defines a test class named `PersonTest` that extends `TestCase` from PHPUnit. Test cases are written as methods within this class:

  ```
  class PersonTest extends TestCase
  ```

- **Test method – testValidPassword**:

  ```
  public function testValidPassword() {
      $person = new Person('testUser@aol.com');
      $this->assertTrue($person->createLogin('ValidPass1!'));
      $this->assertEquals('ValidPass1!', $person->getPassword());
  }
  ```

  This method tests the scenario where a valid password is provided. It creates a new `Person` instance with the email address `testUser@aol.com`, attempts to create a login with the password `ValidPass1!`, and asserts that the `create_login` method returns `true` and that the stored password matches the expected value.

- **Test method – testInvalidShortPassword**:

  ```
  public function testInvalidShortPassword() {
      $person = new Person('testUser@aol.com');
      $this->assertFalse($person->create_login('Short1!'));
      $this->assertNull($person->getPassword());
  }
  ```

  This method tests the scenario where an invalid short password is provided. It asserts that the `create_login` method returns `false` and that the stored password is `null`.

- **Test method – testInvalidNoLowerCasePassword:**

```
public function testInvalidNoLowerCasePassword() {
    $person = new Person('testUser@aol.com');
    $this->assertFalse($person->create_login('UPPERCASE1!'));
    $this->assertNull($person->getPassword());
}
```

This method tests the scenario where the password lacks lowercase characters. It asserts that the `create_login` method returns `false` and that the stored password is `null`.

- **Test method – testInvalidNoUpperCasePassword:**

```
public function testInvalidNoUpperCasePassword() {
    $person = new Person('testUser@aol.com');
    $this->assertFalse($person->create_login('lowercase1!'));
    $this->assertNull($person->getPassword());
}
```

This method tests the scenario where the password lacks uppercase characters. It asserts that the `create_login` method returns `false` and that the stored password is `null`.

- **Test method – testInvalidNoSymbolPassword:**

```
public function testInvalidNoSymbolPassword() {
    $person = new Person('testUser@aol.com');
    $this->assertFalse($person->create_login('NoSymbol123'));
    $this->assertNull($person->getPassword());
}
```

This method tests the scenario where the password lacks symbols. It asserts that the `create_login` method returns `false` and that the stored password is `null`.

These tests cover different scenarios to ensure that the `create_login` method of the `Person` class correctly enforces the specified password requirements. Each test method provides a clear indication of the expected behavior in specific cases, helping to verify the correctness of the `create_login` method.

JUnit

First, we will show the Java representation of the `Person` class:

```
import java.util.regex.Pattern;

public class Person {

    private String firstName;
    private String lastName;
    private String email;
    private String password;
```

```java
    public Person(String email) {
        this.email = email;
    }

    public boolean createLogin(String password) {
        if (isValidPassword(password)) {
            this.password = password;
            return true;
        } else {
            return false;
        }
    }

    private boolean isValidPassword(String password) {
        return password.length() >= 8
                && Pattern.compile("[a-z]").matcher(password).find()
                && Pattern.compile("[A-Z]").matcher(password).find()
                && Pattern.compile("[!@#$%^&*()\\-_=+{};:,<.>]").
                   matcher(password).find();
    }

    public String getPassword() {
        return this.password;
    }
}
```

The following is an example of a JUnit test for a `Person` class, with a `createLogin` method that enforces password requirements:

```java
import org.junit.jupiter.api.Test;
import static org.junit.jupiter.api.Assertions.*;

public class PersonTest {

    @Test
    public void testValidPassword() {
        Person person = new Person("testUser@aol.com");
        assertTrue(person.createLogin("ValidPass1!"));
        assertEquals("ValidPass1!", person.getPassword());
    }

    @Test
    public void testInvalidShortPassword() {
        Person person = new Person("testUser@aol.com");
        assertFalse(person.createLogin("Short1!"));
```

```
        assertNull(person.getPassword());
    }

    @Test
    public void testInvalidNoLowerCasePassword() {
        Person person = new Person("testUser@aol.com");
        assertFalse(person.createLogin("UPPERCASE1!"));
        assertNull(person.getPassword());
    }

    @Test
    public void testInvalidNoUpperCasePassword() {
        Person person = new Person("testUser@aol.com");
        assertFalse(person.createLogin("lowercase1!"));
        assertNull(person.getPassword());
    }

    @Test
    public void testInvalidNoSymbolPassword() {
        Person person = new Person("testUser@aol.com");
        assertFalse(person.createLogin("NoSymbol123"));
        assertNull(person.getPassword());
    }
}
```

Here is an explanation of the Junit code:

- **Annotations**:

  - **@Test**: This indicates that the annotated method is a test method.

- **Test methods**:

  - **testValidPassword**: This tests the scenario where a valid password is provided. It asserts that `create_login` returns `true` and that the stored password matches the expected value.

  - **testInvalidShortPassword**: This tests the scenario where an invalid short password is provided. It asserts that `create_login` returns `false` and that the stored password is `null`.

  - **testInvalidNoLowerCasePassword**: This tests the scenario where the password lacks lowercase characters. It asserts that `create_login` returns `false` and that the stored password is `null`.

  - **testInvalidNoUpperCasePassword**: This tests the scenario where the password lacks uppercase characters. It asserts that `create_login` returns `false` and that the stored password is `null`.

- **testInvalidNoSymbolPassword**: This tests the scenario where the password lacks symbols. It asserts that `create_login` returns `false` and that the stored password is `null`.

To run JUnit tests in Java, you can use an **integrated development environment** (IDE), such as IntelliJ IDEA or Eclipse, or you can run tests from the command line using the `javac` and `java` commands. *Figure 11.1* shows the run test menu in IntelliJ. Here's an essential guide to both approaches:

To use an IDE (IntelliJ IDEA in the JetBrains example), follow these steps:

1. Open your project in IntelliJ IDEA.

2. Make sure your project contains the JUnit library. You can add the JUnit dependency to your project's build configuration.

3. Locate your JUnit test class (e.g., `PersonTest`).

4. Right-click on the test class or a specific test method within the class.

5. Select **Run 'PersonTest'** or **Run 'testValidPassword'** (depending on your selection).

6. Review the test results in the **Run** or **JUnit** tab.

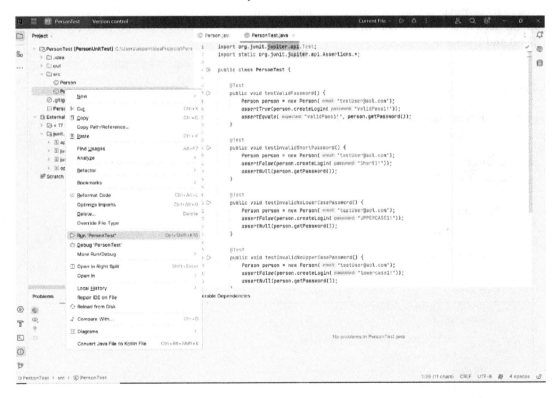

Figure 11.1 – Running a JUnit test in IntelliJ

To use the command line, follow these steps:

1. Compile your source files and test files. Make sure you have both your application code and test code compiled:

    ```
    javac Person.java PersonTest.java
    ```

2. Run the JUnit test using the `org.junit.runner.JUnitCore` class:

    ```
    java -cp .:path/to/junit-4.x.jar:path/to/hamcrest-core-x.x.jar
    org.junit.runner.JUnitCore PersonTest
    ```

    Replace `path/to/junit-4.x.jar` and `path/to/hamcrest-core-x.x.jar` with the actual paths to your JUnit and Hamcrest libraries. Ensure that these JAR files are in your classpath.

3. Review the test results in the console.

> **Note**
>
> The exact commands may vary based on your operating system. If you're using Windows, you might need to use ; instead of : in the classpath, and the file extension might be `.bat` for the JUnit and Hamcrest JARs.

PyUnit

The following is an example of a Python `unittest` (pyUnit) test for a `Person` class, with a `create_login` method that enforces password requirements:

```python
import unittest
import re

class Person:
    def __init__(self, email):
        self.email = email
        self.password = None

    def create_login(self, password):
        """Creates Login"""
        if self.is_valid_password(password):
            self.password = password
            return True
        else:
            return False

    def is_valid_password(self, password):
```

```python
        """Checks if password passes requirements"""
        return len(password) >= 8 \
            and any(c.islower() for c in password) \
            and any(c.isupper() for c in password) \
            and re.search(r'[!@#$%^&*()\-_=+{};:,<.>]', password)

    def get_password(self):
        return self.password


class TestPerson(unittest.TestCase):

    def setUp(self):
        self.person = Person('testUser')

    def test_valid_password(self):
        """Tests a valid password"""
        self.assertTrue(self.person.create_login('ValidPass1!'))
        self.assertEqual('ValidPass1!', self.person.get_password())

    def test_invalid_short_password(self):
        """Tests a password that is too short"""
        self.assertFalse(self.person.create_login('Short1!'))
        self.assertIsNone(self.person.get_password())

    def test_invalid_no_lowercase_password(self):
        """Tests a password with no lowercase"""
        self.assertFalse(self.person.create_login('UPPERCASE1!'))
        self.assertIsNone(self.person.get_password())

    def test_invalid_no_uppercase_password(self):
        """Tests a password with no uppercase"""
        self.assertFalse(self.person.create_login('lowercase1!'))
        self.assertIsNone(self.person.get_password())

    def test_invalid_no_symbol_password(self):
        """Tests a password with no symbol"""
        self.assertFalse(self.person.create_login('NoSymbol123'))
        self.assertIsNone(self.person.get_password())


if __name__ == '__main__':
    unittest.main()
```

With Python, we combined the `unittest` and the `Person` class. Here is an explanation of the combined code:

- The `Person` class is defined with an `__init__` method for initialization, a `create_login` method for password validation, and a `get_password` method to retrieve the stored password

- The `TestPerson` class is a subclass of `unittest.TestCase` and contains test methods (starting with `test_`) to check different scenarios

- The `setUp` method creates an instance of the `Person` class before each test method

- Test methods use assertions (`assertTrue`, `assertFalse`, `assertEqual`, and `assertIsNone`) to check the expected behavior

- `unittest.main()` at the end runs the test cases when the script is executed

You can run this script to execute the tests, providing an output indicating whether each test passed or failed.

Summary

This chapter introduced unit testing. We looked at the principles and advantages of unit testing. Then, we delved into three unit testing examples in the PHP, Java, and Python programming languages.

In the next chapter, we will look at regression testing to ensure that software updates refrain from introducing new security and functional issues.

Self-assessment questions

1. What is the primary purpose of unit testing?

    A. To identify performance issues

    B. To test individual components in isolation

    C. To assess user interface design

    D. To validate an entire application

2. Which of the following is a key benefit of unit testing?

    A. Ensuring a flawless user experience

    B. Improving network performance

    C. Uncovering integration issues

    D. Early detection of bugs

3. What does the term "isolation" mean in the context of unit testing?

    A. Running tests concurrently

    B. Ignoring certain test cases

    C. Testing multiple components together

    D. Testing in a controlled environment

4. In unit testing, what is the role of test cases?

    A. To provide examples of user documentation

    B. To ensure the software is bug-free

    C. To document code structure

    D. To verify the correctness of an entire system

5. How does unit testing contribute to code maintenance?

    A. By eliminating the need for documentation

    B. By outsourcing testing to a separate team

    C. By serving as living documentation

    D. By preventing changes to code

Answers

1. B
2. D
3. B
4. B
5. C

12

Regression Testing

Regression testing is a software testing technique used to verify that changes to an application, such as bug fixes, new features, or code enhancements, have not introduced new defects or caused existing functionality to break. The primary goal of regression testing is to ensure that the software continues to work as expected after each code change, thus maintaining the software's reliability and stability over time.

In this chapter, we're going to cover regression testing by looking at the following main topics:

- Regression testing overview
- Robotic process automation
- Regression testing tools
- Load testing
- UI.Vision RPA
- Example of the enterprise regression tests

By the end of the chapter, we will have a good understanding of the techniques used to ensure changes to code stemming from bug fixes or product enhancements do not create new security vulnerabilities or bugs.

Regression testing overview

Regression testing is software testing that focuses on verifying whether recent code changes have affected the application's existing functionality. It ensures that new code modifications, bug fixes, or enhancements do not introduce new defects, reintroduce old bugs, or break current features. Regression testing aims to maintain the stability and reliability of the software throughout its development life cycle.

Next, we'll provide an overview of regression testing.

Key concepts

Regression testing can feel overwhelming when you first start to utilize the process due to all the components and concepts involved. Next, we will discuss the major concepts:

- **Test suite**: A collection of test cases forms a test suite. The test suite includes new and existing test cases covering various aspects of the software's functionality. These test cases are rerun during regression testing to ensure the recent changes haven't adversely affected the system.

- **Automation**: Regression testing is often automated to facilitate quick and efficient testing. Automated test scripts can be executed repeatedly without manual intervention, making verifying the application's behavior easier after code changes.

- **Continuous Integration (CI) and Continuous Deployment (CD)**: Regression testing is crucial in CI/CD pipelines, where automated tests are run automatically whenever new code changes are integrated into the main code base. CI/CD ensures that any regressions are quickly identified and addressed.

- **Baseline testing**: Initial tests are conducted to establish a baseline for the application's behavior and performance. This baseline becomes the reference point for future regression tests. As the software evolves, the baseline tests are rerun to detect deviations.

- **Selective testing**: Not all test cases must be executed during every regression testing cycle. Testers often prioritize test cases based on the areas affected by recent changes. This selective approach helps save time while still ensuring adequate coverage.

Process

Just like the complexity in the regression testing concepts, the process involves many components or features. Next, we will discuss the major parts of the process of regression testing:

- **Code changes**: Developers make changes to the code base, including bug fixes, feature enhancements, or new functionalities.

- **Test selection**: Testers select relevant test cases from the test suite based on the areas impacted by the code changes. The appropriate tests ensure that testing efforts are focused on the affected functionalities.

- **Test execution**: The selected test cases are executed manually or through automated testing tools. We will discuss several automated testing tools later in this chapter. The goal is to verify that the recent code changes have not introduced defects or negatively affected existing features.

- **Analysis and debugging**: If any test cases fail, the development team investigates the issues to identify the cause of failure. The investigation may involve debugging the code and making necessary corrections. There may be different teams that handle different types of bugs, such as security versus functionality.

- **Regression test suite maintenance:** The regression test suite is periodically reviewed and updated to accommodate new functionalities and changes in the application. The review ensures that the test suite remains relevant and effective over time.

Benefits

The good news is that with the complexity comes many benefits of regression testing. Next, we will discuss the benefits at a high level:

- **Early defect detection:** Regression testing helps catch defects early in the development process, preventing the introduction of bugs into the production environment.

- **Stability assurance:** By verifying existing functionality after code changes, regression testing ensures the overall stability and reliability of the software.

- **Automation efficiency:** Automated regression testing allows for the quick and frequent execution of test cases, providing rapid feedback to developers and reducing the time and effort required for manual testing. Automated testing has drawbacks mainly around costs and the complexity of setting up and maintaining the testing environment.

- **Supports Agile development:** Regression testing aligns well with Agile development methodologies, where frequent code changes are expected. It allows for continuous validation of software integrity during iterative development.

- **Risk mitigation:** Continuous regression testing helps mitigate the risk of unintended side effects caused by code changes, improving overall software quality.

In summary, regression testing is essential in software development to ensure that code changes do not negatively impact existing functionality. It plays a crucial role in maintaining the reliability and quality of software throughout its life cycle.

Robotic process automation

Robotic Process Automation (RPA) and regression testing are two distinct concepts. Still, they can intersect in specific scenarios, particularly when automating repetitive tasks and ensuring the stability of software applications. Let's explore the relationship between RPA and regression testing.

RPA involves using software robots or "bots" to automate rule-based, repetitive tasks within business processes. These tasks are typically manual, time-consuming, and prone to human error. By automating such tasks, RPA aims to increase efficiency, accuracy, and productivity. RPA is commonly used in data entry, data extraction, invoice processing, report generation, and other routine business processes involving interacting with digital systems. RPA bots interact with applications in a way similar to how humans do. They can mimic mouse clicks, keyboard inputs, and data entry to perform tasks within the UI of applications.

The intersection of RPA and regression testing

RPA and regression are used together in several ways to improve the effectiveness in the discovery of bugs and security vulnerabilities introduced in code changes:

- **Automating regression testing with RPA**: RPA tools can be leveraged to automate certain aspects of regression testing, especially when testing involves repetitive, rule-based tasks. RPA bots can simulate user interactions with the application's interface to execute regression test cases.

- **Continuous integration and RPA**: In a CI environment, RPA can be integrated into the build and deployment pipeline to automate end-to-end regression testing. The end-to-end testing ensures that critical business processes, which may involve RPA, are validated automatically whenever code changes occur.

- **Data migration and validation**: RPA can automate data migration tasks and validate data accuracy in the target system. The automation aligns with the objectives of regression testing, ensuring that data-related functionalities continue to work correctly after changes to the system.

- **Enhancing test coverage**: RPA can help expand test coverage by automating tests that involve complex interactions with external systems, databases, or third-party applications. The expanded tests can complement traditional regression testing efforts.

- **UI testing**: RPA tools are well suited for automating tests that involve interactions with the application's UI. The interaction includes validating the correctness of user workflows and ensuring that UIs remain functional after updates.

While RPA and regression testing have different primary purposes, there can be synergy in their application, especially in scenarios where automation is beneficial for repetitive tasks and comprehensive testing is required to maintain the integrity of business processes and software applications. Integrating RPA into the regression testing strategy can contribute to a more robust and efficient testing process.

Regression testing tools

Various tools are available for regression testing, ranging from general-purpose test automation tools to more specialized solutions. The choice of regression testing tool often depends on factors such as the type of application, the technology stack, team preferences, and budget considerations. Here are some popular regression testing tools:

- **Selenium**:

  - **Language support**: Java, C#, Python, Ruby, JavaScript, and Kotlin.

  - **Description**: Selenium is a widely used open source framework for web application testing. It supports multiple browsers and can be used for functional and regression testing. Selenium WebDriver allows for browser automation.

- **JUnit**:

  - **Language support**: Java.

  - **Description**: JUnit is a popular testing framework for Java. While it is primarily used for unit testing, it can also be employed for regression testing when combined with other tools or frameworks. It follows the xUnit style of testing.

- **TestNG**:

  - **Language support**: Java.

  - **Description**: TestNG is a testing framework for Java inspired by JUnit but with additional features. It supports parallel test execution, data-driven testing, and configuration flexibility, making it suitable for regression testing.

- **NUnit**:

  - **Language support**: C#.

  - **Description**: NUnit is a unit testing framework for the .NET platform, particularly for C#. It is widely used for both the unit and regression testing of .NET applications.

- **xUnit.net**:

  - **Language support**: .NET languages (C# and F#).

  - **Description**: xUnit.net is a modern testing framework for .NET that supports unit testing and can be extended to regression testing. It follows a structure similar to that of other xUnit frameworks.

- **TestComplete**:

  - **Language support**: JavaScript, Python, VBScript, JScript, DelphiScript, and C++Script.

  - **Description**: TestComplete is a commercial test automation tool that supports desktop, web, and mobile application testing. It offers a record-and-playback feature along with script-based testing.

- **Jenkins**:

  - **Language support**: Dependent on the testing tools integrated.

  - **Description**: Jenkins is an open source automation server that supports building, testing, and deploying code. While Jenkins is not a testing tool, it integrates with various regression testing tools and frameworks, making it a crucial part of CI and regression testing pipelines.

- **Appium**:

  - **Language support**: Java, C#, Python, Ruby, JavaScript, and Kotlin.

  - **Description**: Appium is an open source automation tool for mobile applications on Android and iOS platforms. It supports native, hybrid, and mobile web applications.

- **SoapUI**:

  - **Language support**: Groovy (scripting language).

  - **Description**: SoapUI is a widely used open source tool for testing SOAP and RESTful web services. It allows for functional, regression, and performance testing of APIs.

- **Postman**:

  - **Language support**: N/A (uses its own scripting language).

  - **Description**: Postman is a popular API testing tool that enables the creation and execution of automated tests for APIs. It also supports automated testing for GraphQL, Redis, and WebSocket APIs.

When choosing a regression testing tool, consider factors such as the type of application you are testing, the testing environment, integration capabilities, ease of use, and community support. Tools such as Selenium, JUnit, and TestNG are commonly used to achieve comprehensive regression testing for web applications.

Load testing

Regression and load testing serve different purposes in the software testing life cycle, but they can complement each other to ensure an application's overall quality and performance. Let's explore the distinctions between regression testing and load testing, as well as how they can be integrated into a comprehensive testing strategy:

- **Purpose**: Load testing assesses the application's performance under expected and peak load conditions. It aims to identify performance bottlenecks, scalability issues, and potential points of failure when many users or transactions are processed simultaneously. Regression testing mainly focuses on changes in performance introduced with code changes.

- **Scope**: Load testing simulates realistic user scenarios, including various types of transactions, user interactions, and system behaviors. It helps evaluate the system's response time, throughput, and resource utilization under different load levels. Like the purpose, the difference is that regression is focused on changes to these items with the latest version of the code.

- **Testing techniques**: Load testing is often automated and involves specialized load testing tools. These tools simulate virtual users or clients to generate realistic traffic and measure the system's performance metrics. Regression testing can often utilize standard outputs from a system such as reports, exports, or web pages to compare changes.

- **Frequency**: Load testing is typically performed at specific stages of the software development life cycle, such as before a significant release or during the preparation for anticipated high-traffic events. It may not be executed as frequently as regression tests with every code change.

Next, we will discuss how regression testing and load testing can be combined to reduce issues introduced in the code changes.

Integration and complementarity

The following are some benefits of the combination of load and regression testing:

- **Preventing performance regressions**: Regression tests ensure the functional stability of the application, but they may not directly address performance-related issues. Combining regression testing with load testing helps prevent performance regressions by identifying potential bottlenecks early in development.

- **CI and load testing**: Integrating load testing into CI pipelines ensures that performance considerations are part of the overall testing strategy. Automated load tests can be triggered during the build and deployment process.

- **Scalability assessment**: Load testing is precious for assessing the scalability of an application. It helps determine how well the system can handle increasing users, transactions, or data volume.

- **Realistic user scenarios**: Load tests can benefit from realistic user scenarios created during regression testing. The scenarios used for load testing should encompass functional and performance aspects to evaluate the application comprehensively.

- **Identifying resource bottlenecks**: Load testing tools can help identify resource bottlenecks, such as database issues or inefficient code, that may not be evident in typical regression testing scenarios.

In summary, while regression testing focuses on ensuring the functional stability of an application, load testing assesses its performance under various load conditions to ensure the performance meets the specified non-functional requirements. Integrating regression and load testing into a testing strategy provides a more comprehensive approach to delivering a reliable and performant software application.

UI.Vision RPA

UI.Vision RPA (formerly Kantu Selenium IDE) is an open source browser extension that provides a browser automation and web scraping solution. It is designed for creating and running Selenium-like scripts for web browser automation tasks, and it can be used for various purposes, including regression testing. Here's how UI.Vision RPA can be used for regression testing:

- **Record and replay**: UI.Vision RPA allows users to record their interactions with a web application, creating a script that can later be replayed to automate repetitive tasks. The record and replay functionality is beneficial for creating regression test scripts that mimic user interactions.

- **Selenium-compatible**: The tool is built on Selenium WebDriver, making it compatible with Selenium commands. If you are familiar with Selenium and transitioning to UI.Vision RPA for regression testing may be relatively seamless.

- **Scripting support**: While UI.Vision RPA provides a simple record-and-replay interface and supports scripting using the Selenium IDE script format. The scripting allows users to add custom logic and enhance their regression tests.

- **Cross-browser testing**: UI.Vision RPA can be used for cross-browser testing as it supports various web browsers, including Chrome, Firefox, and Edge. Cross-browser testing ensures that web applications work consistently across different browsers.

- **Data-driven testing**: UI.Vision RPA supports data-driven testing by allowing users to import external data (e.g., CSV or Excel files) and use that data within their scripts. Data-driven testing helps run the same test with different input values.

- **Integration with CI**: UI.Vision RPA scripts can be integrated into CI/CD pipelines for automated regression testing as part of the development workflow. The integration ensures that tests are executed regularly, providing quick feedback on code changes.

The steps to use UI.Vision RPA for regression testing are as follows:

1. **Install the browser extension**: Install the UI.Vision RPA browser extension for the browser you want to automate (e.g., Chrome, Firefox, and Edge).

2. **Record regression test**: Use the record feature to interact with your web application and perform the actions you want to include in your regression test.

3. **Enhance script (optional)**: You can enhance the generated script with additional commands or custom logic using the Selenium IDE script format.

4. **Data-driven testing (optional)**: If your regression test requires different input values, you can set up data-driven testing by importing external data files.

5. **Run regression test**: Execute the regression test manually or integrate it into your CI/CD pipeline to run automatically.

6. **Review the test results to identify any failures or regressions**: UI.Vision RPA provides logs and reports to help diagnose issues.

Here are some considerations when utilizing UI.Vision for regression testing:

- **Maintenance**: Keep in mind that UI.Vision RPA scripts may need updates if there are changes to the web application's UI. Regularly review and update scripts to ensure they remain accurate.

- **Cross-browser testing**: Test your web application across different browsers to ensure compatibility.

- **Data security**: Be cautious when dealing with sensitive data in regression tests and ensure that test environments are appropriately isolated from production. Data entered in test scripts may include usernames, passwords, credit card numbers, or other sensitive data that should be protected.

While UI.Vision RPA is a versatile tool for web automation, consider your specific project requirements and whether UI.Vision RPA aligns well with your regression testing needs. I included the deep dive into UI.Vision here because it will be easy for you to install and gain insight into the regression testing concepts. Depending on the complexity and scope of your tests, you may also explore other Selenium-based frameworks or tools.

Example of the enterprise regression tests

Throughout this book, we will build a secure design for an event ticketing system. Envision a software system that allows a box office or a website to sell tickets to a famous musical concert or theatre event. We will utilize two tools that are easier for you to install and experiment with for the regression testing. These tools are UI.Vision RPA and Postman. We created a few elementary segments of program code to show the process. The first set of code we want to look at is a simple HTML form to allow a user to select seats:

```
<form action="addtickets.php" method="post">
    <label for="tkts">Choose your seats:</label>

    <select name="tkts[]" multiple>
      <option value="AA101">AA101</option>
      <option value="AA102">AA102</option>
      <option value="AA103">AA103</option>
      <option value="AA104">AA104</option>
      <option value="AA105">AA105</option>
      <option value="AA106">AA106</option>
      <option value="AA107">AA107</option>
      <option value="AA108">AA108</option>
    </select><br>
  <input type="submit" value="Submit">

</form>
```

This simple HTML form has a selection box where the user can select seats they would like to purchase. The selection box allows for multiple selections. A submit button will call simple PHP server-side code called `addtickets.php`. In the code, we use one of the PHP filter constants, `FILTER_SANITIZE_STRING`. This filter will remove tags and HTML-encode double and single quotes. There are dozens of filters available depending on the specific requirements of the input. The code is displayed next:

```php
<?php

foreach($_REQUEST["tkts"] as $tkt)
{
    $newtkt = filter_var($tkt, FILTER_SANITIZE_STRING);
    $response = file_get_contents('http://test.alliance.biz/lockseat.
      php?seat=' . $newtkt);
    if(!strpos($response, 'Locked'))
        echo "Warning Seat $newtkt Could Not Be Added To The Basket!</
          br>";
}
?>
```

This simple server-side code looks through the seats selected. It sanitizes the input for each seat to ensure no scripts are in the text. For each seat, it calls a simple REST web service to lock the seat. For simplicity, we do not include error handling for network or server-related errors such as timeouts or invalid responses.

We can automate the testing of clicking on different seats with the UI.Vision RPA tool. The following is a simple UI.Vision RPA script that clicks on the AA101 seat and hits the submit button:

```json
{
  "Name": "Regression Test for Add Tickets",
  "CreationDate": "2023-12-21",
  "Commands": [
    {
      "Command": "open",
      "Target": "http://test.alliance.biz/addtickets.html",
      "Value": "",
      "Description": ""
    },
    {
      "Command": "addSelection",
      "Target": "name=tkts[]",
      "Value": "label=AA101",
      "Description": ""
    },
```

```
{
  "Command": "clickAndWait",
  "Target": "xpath=/html/body/form/input",
  "Value": "",
  "Targets": [
    "xpath=/html/body/form/input",
    "xpath=//input[@value='Submit']",
    "xpath=//input",
    "css=body > form > input"
  ],
  "Description": ""
}
    ]
}
```

The LockSeat REST web service can be tested separately with the Postman tool. The following is the code for our simple web service:

```php
<?php
$seat = $_REQUEST["seat"];
$mysqli = new mysqli("localhost", "u500438778_test", "Snow1234",
"u500438778_test");
$call = mysqli_prepare($mysqli, 'CALL lock_seat(?, @message)');
mysqli_stmt_bind_param($call, 's', $seat);
mysqli_stmt_execute($call);
$select = mysqli_query($mysqli, 'SELECT @message');
$result = mysqli_fetch_assoc($select);
$return_value = $result['@message'];
print "procedure returned $return_value\n";
?>
```

The code in the web service is just a simple wrapper for a MySQL-stored procedure. We connect to the database in the code, set up a prepared statement, and call the web service. This PHP code uses the MySQLi library to connect to the database, as discussed in *Chapter 10* to minimize the risk of SQL injection. *Figure 12.1* shows a screenshot of Postman with a set of tests that call the LockSeat web service and test whether the response time is under 200 ms, no error was returned, and whether the Locked string was included in the results.

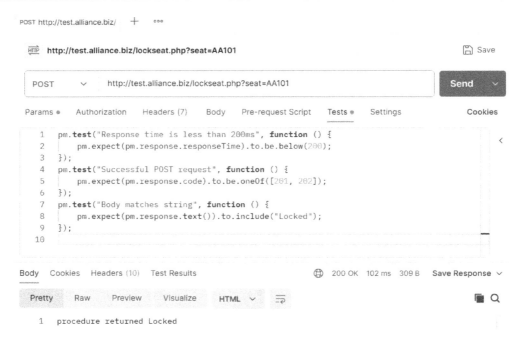

Figure 12.1 – Postman tests on the LockSeat web service

These few applied examples of regression testing are just a start to developing a robust regression test. In a real scenario, every activity and web service would need code coverage in your regression tests.

Summary

This chapter introduced regression testing. We looked at regression testing in general, including the process and benefits. After that, we looked at RPA and load testing. We discussed several tools available for both regression testing and RPA. We finished the chapter by showing the use of UI.Vision RPA and Postman on a simple set of calls across partitions in our application.

In the next chapter, we will look at integration testing and ways to test early and ensure the components of our software system work together.

Self-assessment questions

1. What is regression testing primarily concerned with?

    A. Testing previously working functionality after changes

    B. Testing the software for defects before release

    C. Testing new features of the software

    D. Testing user interfaces for usability

2. When is regression testing typically performed in the software development lifecycle?

   A. Throughout the entire development process

   B. Before unit testing

   C. After system testing

   D. During acceptance testing

3. What is the primary difference between regression testing and functional testing?

   A. Regression testing occurs before development, while functional testing occurs after development.

   B. Regression testing focuses on new features, while functional testing focuses on existing ones.

   C. Regression testing verifies that changes do not adversely affect existing functionality, while functional testing verifies specific features against requirements.

   D. Regression testing is manual, while functional testing is automated.

4. Which of the following is NOT a typical approach to regression testing?

   A. Repeating only the failed test cases from the previous test cycle

   B. Testing only the new features introduced in the software

   C. Retesting all test cases from scratch

   D. Selecting representative test cases from the entire test suite

5. In which situation would selective regression testing be most beneficial?

   A. When the software undergoes major architectural changes

   B. When the software undergoes minor changes

   C. When the software is tested for the first time

   D. When the software has no previous test cases

Answers

1. A

2. A

3. C

4. B

5. B

13

Integration, System, and Acceptance Testing

Integration testing is a software testing technique that focuses on verifying the interactions and interfaces between different components or modules of a software application. The primary goal of integration testing is to ensure that the integrated components work together as expected when combined into a complete system. It helps identify issues related to data flow, communication between modules, and the overall behavior of the integrated software.

In this chapter, we're going to cover integration testing by looking at the following main topics:

- Types of tests
- Mocks
- Stubs
- Examples of enterprise integration tests
- System testing
- Acceptance testing

By the end of this chapter, you will understand the types and benefits of integration testing. You will also be able to differentiate integration testing from the earlier unit testing and regression testing we discussed.

Types of integration tests

Integration testing is a crucial phase in software development where individual units or components are combined and tested as a group. The primary goal is to ensure that the integrated components work as expected when interacting. There are a number of types of integration tests, each focusing on different aspects of the software architecture. Next, we will drill into some common types of integration tests:

- **Big Bang integration testing**: In this approach, all components are integrated simultaneously, and the system is tested. The Big Bang method is typically used for smaller projects or when the components are loosely coupled.

- **Incremental integration testing**: The system is built and tested incrementally, with new components integrated individually. Incremental integration suits larger projects, allowing for continuous testing and verification of newly integrated components.

- **Top-down integration testing**: Testing begins with the highest-level modules; lower-level modules are integrated and tested incrementally. Top-down integration testing effectively identifies issues in higher-level modules early in the testing process.

- **Bottom-up integration testing**: Testing begins with the lowest-level modules, and higher-level modules are integrated and tested incrementally. Bottom-up allows for early testing of core functionalities and can be beneficial when higher-level modules depend on lower-level modules.

- **Functional integration testing**: This focuses on verifying that the integrated components work together to achieve specific functionalities or features. Functional integration ensures the system behaves as expected when different components interact to deliver particular functionalities.

- **Non-functional integration testing**: This evaluates non-functional aspects such as performance, security, and reliability in an integrated environment. Non-functional integration testing verifies the system meets non-functional requirements when multiple components interact.

- **Interface testing**: This tests the communication and data exchange between different components or systems to ensure seamless integration. Interface testing ensures that interfaces between components are well-defined and operate as expected.

- **Concurrency testing**: This focuses on identifying issues related to the simultaneous execution of multiple components or processes. Concurrency testing ensures the system can handle concurrent access and operations without deadlocks or data corruption.

- **Dependency testing**: This verifies that components or modules do not have unexpected dependencies on each other. Dependency testing identifies and resolves issues related to dependencies that could lead to system failures or unexpected behavior.

- **Stub testing**: This involves replacing a called module with a simulated or stub module to test the calling module. Stub testing is practical when specific components are unavailable, allowing testing to proceed with simulated functionality.

- **Smoke testing**: This verifies that the major functionalities of the integrated system work as expected after initial integration. Smoke testing provides a quick check to ensure the core functionalities are operational before deeper testing.

Choosing the appropriate type of integration testing depends on the project's complexity, the development methodology, and the specific goals of the testing phase. In practice, a combination of these testing types is often employed to comprehensively validate a software system's integrated components.

Mocks

In software integration testing, mocks are objects or components that simulate the behavior of natural system components or dependencies. The purpose of mocks is to isolate the component being tested from its dependencies, allowing the testing focus to be on the component's functionality in isolation. Mocks help create controlled environments for integration testing, and they are instrumental when testing components that interact with external systems, databases, or services.

Here are some key concepts related to the use of mocks in software integration testing:

- **Mock objects**: A mock object is a simulated object that mimics the behavior of a real object or component. It is designed to respond to method calls or requests in a predefined manner. During integration testing, mock objects, such as external services or databases, replace actual dependencies. They ensure that the component under test interacts correctly with its dependencies.

- **Purpose of mocks in integration testing**: Mocks help isolate the tested component from its external dependencies, allowing for more controlled testing environments. By defining how mocks respond to specific inputs, tests become more deterministic. The isolation is crucial for reproducing test scenarios consistently.

- **Manual versus automated mocks**: Manual mocks are handcrafted mock objects developers create to simulate specific behaviors. These are often used when testing is done in a controlled environment. Automated mocks are generated or configured automatically using mocking frameworks. These frameworks allow for the creation of mock objects with predefined behaviors.

- **Mocking frameworks**: Various mocking frameworks are available for different programming languages, such as Mockito for Java, Moq for C#, and unittest.mock for Python. Mocking frameworks provide features for creating, configuring, and verifying the behavior of mock objects. They often support the creation of partial mocks, where only specific methods of an object are mocked.

- **Behavior verification**: Mocks are often used for behavior verification. The verification involves checking that the tested component interacts with its dependencies by verifying the calls made to the mock objects. An example is verifying that a method was called several times or with particular parameters.

- **State verification versus behavior verification**: State verification involves checking the internal state of an object after an operation. State verification is less common in integration testing, where the focus is on the interaction between components. Behavior verification ensures that the correct methods are called with the expected parameters.

- **Mocking external services**: When testing a component that interacts with external services (e.g., REST APIs), mocks can be used to simulate the behavior of those services without making actual network requests. The advantage of this approach is that it reduces dependencies on external services, making tests faster and more reliable.

- **Mocking databases**: Mocks can simulate database queries and responses when testing components that interact with databases. An advantage of mocking databases is that tests can be executed without affecting the database, and specific scenarios (e.g., error conditions) can be simulated.

Using mocks in integration testing helps developers and testers create more robust and reliable tests by controlling the behavior of external dependencies. It allows for identifying issues related to component interactions while maintaining a controlled and deterministic testing environment. We will drill into an example database component mock in our continued enterprise ticketing example. It is essential to recognize that mocks can be used in all application partitions.

Stubs

In software integration testing, stubs are components or modules that simulate the behavior of natural components or dependencies. Stubs replace components or modules that are external to the unit being tested. The primary purpose of using stubs is to create a controlled testing environment and to isolate the unit under test from its external dependencies. Stubs provide simple predefined responses to requests made by the unit being tested, allowing developers to verify that the unit integrates correctly with its dependencies.

Here are some key concepts related to the use of stubs in integration software testing:

- **Stub definition**: A stub is a minimal implementation of a component or module that provides predefined responses to calls being tested by the unit. It is a temporary replacement for the actual component to isolate the unit under test during integration testing. Stubs help create a controlled environment for testing and allow the unit under test to interact with simulated versions of its dependencies.

- **Isolation of units**: Stubs isolate the unit under test from external dependencies. This isolation ensures that integration testing focuses on the unit's behavior rather than the behavior of its dependencies.

- **Manual versus automated stubs**: Manual stubs are handcrafted stubs developers create to simulate specific behaviors. Manual stubs are often used when testing in a controlled environment. Automated stubs are generated or configured automatically using stubbing frameworks. These frameworks allow for the creation of stubs with predefined behaviors.

- **Stubbing frameworks**: Various stubbing frameworks are available for different programming languages. Examples include Mockito for Java, Sinon for JavaScript, and unittest.mock for Python. Stubbing frameworks provide features for creating, configuring, and verifying the behavior of stubs. They often support the creation of partial stubs, where only specific methods of an object are stubbed.

- **Stubs for external services**: When testing a component that interacts with external services (e.g., web services, APIs), stubs can simulate the behavior of those services without making actual network requests.

- **Stubs for databases**: Stubs can simulate database queries and responses when testing components that interact with databases.

- **Behavior of stubs**: Stubs provide predefined responses to method calls or requests made by the tested unit. Developers typically configure these responses to simulate various scenarios.

- **Limitations of stubs**: Stubs may provide simplified or static behavior and might not fully replicate the complexity of the components they replace. This limitation can impact the realism of the test scenarios.

- **Isolation**: Stubs help isolate the unit under test, enabling developers to focus on specific functionalities without being affected by the behavior of external components.

- **Controlled testing**: Stubs provide a controlled testing environment where developers can simulate different scenarios and responses for integration testing.

Using stubs in integration testing is particularly useful when external components are not yet available or when there is a need to control specific conditions for testing purposes. It allows for the systematic and controlled evaluation of how a unit interacts with its dependencies without relying on the full implementation of those dependencies. We will drill into an example of a stub in our continued enterprise ticketing example. It is essential to recognize that stubs can be used in all application partitions, just like the mocks we discussed earlier.

Examples of enterprise integration testing

Throughout this book, we will build a secure design for an event ticketing system. Envision a software system that allows a box office or a website to sell tickets to a popular music concert or theatre event. In *Chapter 12*, we looked at the integration testing of a web service called a MySQL stored procedure, called `lock_seats`. A significant challenge of developing large software systems is the complexity that comes from the dependency between subsystems. To allow us to test early, we create a stub in MySQL with a hardcode output response dependent on the input:

```
DELIMITER //
CREATE PROCEDURE lock_seats(IN inseat CHAR(6),OUT result VARCHAR(255))
BEGIN
  IF inseat = "AA101" THEN
```

```
    SET result = "Seat AA101 Locked";
  ELSE
    SET result = CONCAT('Seat ', inseat, ' Already Taken');   END IF;
END //
```

If we have the stored procedure developed, we may want to create a mock so that the state of the database is not changed. In our implementation, the stored procedure inserts a record into a table named `locked_seats`. We show the implementation next:

```
DELIMITER //
CREATE PROCEDURE lock_seats(IN inseat CHAR(6),OUT result VARCHAR(255))
BEGIN
  INSERT INTO locked_seats (seat) VALUES (inseat);
  IF @ROW_COUNT() = 1 THEN
    SET result = CONCAT('Seat ', inseat, ' Locked');
  ELSE
    SET result = CONCAT('Seat ', inseat, ' Already Taken');   END IF;
END //
```

Unfortunately, the state of the database is changed with the insert, which requires further actions in the workflow to either confirm or remove the lock. In testing, we can create a mock that removes the lock record so the procedure can be called again without the complete workflow:

```
DELIMITER //
CREATE PROCEDURE lock_seats (IN inseat CHAR(6),OUT result
VARCHAR(255))
BEGIN
  INSERT INTO locked_seats (seat) VALUES (inseat);
  IF ROW_COUNT() = 1 THEN
    SET result = CONCAT('Seat ', inseat, ' Locked');
    DELETE FROM locked_seats WHERE seat = inseat;
  ELSE
    SET result = CONCAT('Seat ', inseat, ' Already Taken');
  END IF;
END //
```

We have shown a few simple examples here of mocks and stubs. These are small examples that are easy to show in a book, but mocks and stubs can be complex classes or components with many method and attribute signatures where only one is utilized in the testing.

System testing

System testing is a crucial phase in the software testing process, where the entire integrated software system is tested to ensure that it behaves as expected and meets the specified requirements. What follows is a general overview of the critical aspects of system testing for a software application:

1. **Test environment setup**:

   - Establish a dedicated testing environment that closely mimics the production environment
   - Ensure that all required hardware, software, and network configurations are in place

2. **Test planning**:

   - Develop a comprehensive system test plan that outlines the scope, objectives, resources, schedule, and criteria for success
   - Identify the test scenarios and cases based on the system requirements and specifications

3. **Functional testing**:

   - Verify that the software functions as intended according to the specified requirements
   - Test each feature and functionality to ensure they work individually and in conjunction

4. **Performance testing**:

   - Evaluate the system's performance under various conditions, such as load, stress, and scalability
   - Measure and optimize response times, throughput, and resource utilization

5. **Security testing**:

   - Assess the application's security measures to identify vulnerabilities and ensure data protection
   - Test for potential security breaches, unauthorized access, and data integrity

6. **Usability testing**:

   - Evaluate the user interface and overall user experience to ensure it is intuitive and user-friendly
   - Confirm that the application meets usability and accessibility standards

7. **Compatibility testing**:

   - Test the software across browsers, operating systems, and devices to ensure compatibility
   - Address any issues related to platform-specific behaviors

8. **Documentation verification**:

- Confirm that all documentation, including user manuals and technical documentation, is accurate and up to date

9. **Error handling and logging**:

- Evaluate how the application handles errors and exceptions
- Review the effectiveness of error messages and ensure proper logging for troubleshooting

10. **Data integrity testing**:

- Verify that data is stored, retrieved, and processed accurately within the system
- Test data integrity during various operations and transactions

11. **Installation and configuration testing**:

- Ensure that the installation and configuration processes are smooth and error-free
- Test the application's behavior when installed or configured in different environments

12. **Test completion and reporting**:

- Summarize the results of the system testing phase in a comprehensive test summary report
- Provide detailed information on identified issues, their severity, and any recommendations for improvement

It's important to note that the specific activities and focus areas of system testing may vary depending on the nature of the software application, industry requirements, and project constraints. The goal is to ensure the software is reliable and secure and performs as intended in real-world scenarios.

Acceptance testing

Acceptance testing is the phase in the software testing process where the software is evaluated to determine whether it satisfies the specified requirements and is ready for deployment. End users or stakeholders typically conduct this type of testing to ensure the software meets their expectations and business needs. Acceptance testing is often the final phase before the software is released.

There are two main types of acceptance testing: **User Acceptance Testing** (**UAT**) and **Operational Acceptance Testing** (**OAT**). Each type comes from a different perspective and together they give a better understanding of software functionality and resiliency.

User Acceptance Testing (UAT):

- **Objective:** To validate that the software meets the business requirements from the end user's perspective

- **Participants:** End users or end user representatives, business analysts, and other stakeholders

- **Execution:** Users perform real-world scenarios and tasks to assess the software's functionality, usability, and compliance with business requirements

Here are the types:

- **Alpha testing:** Testing is performed by a select end user group in a controlled environment

- **Beta testing:** A pre-release software version is available to a broader audience to gather feedback

Operational Acceptance Testing (OAT):

- **Objective:** To verify that the software can be smoothly operated and managed in its intended production environment

- **Participants:** System administrators, IT operations staff, and other personnel responsible for deploying and maintaining the software

- **Execution:** Focuses on installation, configuration, performance, reliability, and disaster recovery procedures

Here are the types:

- **Installation testing:** Ensures the software can be installed and configured correctly

- **Performance testing:** Verifies that the software performs well under expected workloads

- **Security testing:** Validates the software's security measures and compliance with security policies

- **Backup and recovery testing:** Ensures data can be backed up and restored effectively

What follows are the critical steps in the acceptance testing process:

1. **Test planning:** Develop a test plan outlining the scope, objectives, schedule, and resources for acceptance testing

2. **Test case design:** Create test scenarios and test cases based on business requirements and user stories

3. **Test execution:** Users execute test cases to validate the software's functionality, usability, and compliance with business needs

4. **Defect reporting:** Identify and report any defects or discrepancies between the expected and actual behavior

5. **Defect resolution:** Developers address and fix reported defects, and the fixes are re-tested by users

6. **Approval and sign-off**: Once users are satisfied with the software's performance and functionality, they formally approve its release

7. **Documentation**: Update documentation based on the final accepted version, including user manuals and release notes

Acceptance testing provides a level of comfort to the development team and stakeholders that the software is ready for production. It helps ensure that the software meets technical specifications and aligns with business goals and user expectations.

Summary

This chapter introduced integration testing. We looked at different integration tests used in software testing. Next, we drilled into stubs and mocks in integration testing. We developed some simple examples of mocks and stubs used in our enterprise entertainment ticketing system. We concluded with a discussion on system and user acceptance testing.

In the next chapter, we will drill into penetration testing to discover security flaws we did not model in earlier phases of the software development lifecycle.

Self-assessment questions

1. Which of the following best describes integration testing?

    A. Testing the system as a whole to ensure it meets the specified requirements.

    B. Testing individual components or modules in isolation to ensure they function correctly.

    C. Testing the integration of different systems or subsystems to verify that they work together as intended.

    D. Testing the user interface and user interactions to ensure usability.

2. What is the primary objective of system testing?

    A. To identify defects in the system's design and architecture.

    B. To ensure that each individual component works correctly.

    C. To verify that the system meets its specified requirements and functions as expected.

    D. To evaluate the system's performance under various conditions.

3. Acceptance testing is typically performed by:

    A. Developers

    B. Quality Assurance (QA) team

    C. End users or stakeholders

    D. System architects

4. Which of the following is NOT typically included in acceptance testing?

    A. Alpha testing

    B. Beta testing

    C. Usability testing

    D. Unit testing

5. During integration testing, stubs and drivers are used to:

    A. Simulate the behavior of components outside the tested unit.

    B. Test the integration of different modules.

    C. Verify that the system meets its specified requirements.

    D. Monitor system performance under load.

Answers

1. C

2. C

3. C

4. D

5. A

14

Software Penetration Testing

Penetration testing, often called "pen testing," is a cybersecurity practice that involves simulating real-world cyberattacks on software systems, networks, and applications to identify vulnerabilities and weaknesses that malicious actors might exploit. The primary goal of penetration testing is to assess the security posture of a system and help organizations strengthen their defenses by addressing any identified vulnerabilities.

In this chapter, we're going to cover penetration testing by looking at the following main topics:

- Types of tests
- Phases
- Tools
- Example of an enterprise penetration test report

By the end of this chapter, you will have a good understanding of the purpose, types, and phases of penetration testing, along with the many tools available to assist in the process.

Types of tests

There are various types of penetration testing in software, each focusing on different security aspects. Here are some common types:

- **Black box testing**:

    - Testers have no prior knowledge of the target system

    - Simulates an external hacker with no insider information

    - Helps identify vulnerabilities that can be exploited without internal knowledge

- **White box testing**:

  - Testers have complete knowledge of the target system's internal workings
  - Simulates an attack by someone with insider information
  - Helps identify vulnerabilities that might be exploited with insider knowledge

- **Gray box testing**:

  - Testers have partial knowledge of the target system in terms of some information on the environment, such as the OS or compiler, but no access to source code
  - Simulates an attack by someone with limited insider information
  - Aims to find vulnerabilities that could be exploited with partial knowledge

- **Web application testing**:

  - Focuses on identifying vulnerabilities in web applications
  - Includes testing for common web application security issues such as SQL injection, cross-site scripting (XSS), and security misconfigurations

- **Network penetration testing**:

  - Evaluates the security of a network infrastructure
  - Identifies vulnerabilities in routers, switches, firewalls, and other network devices

- **Mobile application testing**:

  - Concentrates on security issues specific to mobile applications
  - Examines vulnerabilities related to data storage, communication, and authentication

- **Social engineering testing**:

  - Involves manipulating individuals to divulge confidential information
  - Tests the human element of security, such as phishing attacks and impersonation

- **Wireless network testing**:

  - Evaluate the security of wireless networks
  - Identifies vulnerabilities in Wi-Fi networks and Bluetooth or cellular networks and any associated devices

- **Physical penetration testing:**

  - Simulates a physical attack on the premises

  - Tests the effectiveness of physical security measures

- **IoT (internet of things) testing:**

  - Focuses on security issues in IoT devices and ecosystems

  - Identifies vulnerabilities in smart devices and their communication protocols

It's important to note that the penetration testing type depends on the specific needs and concerns of the organization or system being tested. Additionally, a combination of these testing types may be employed to assess overall security comprehensively.

Phases

Software penetration testing typically involves several phases to ensure a comprehensive evaluation of the security posture of a system or application. The exact phases may vary depending on the methodology or framework followed, but the following are commonly recognized phases in penetration testing:

1. **Pre-engagement:**

   - Scope Definition: Clearly define the scope of the penetration test, specifying what systems, networks, and applications are within the testing boundaries.

   - Rules of engagement: Establish rules and guidelines for the testing team, including what actions are permitted, the testing timeframe, and any constraints.

2. **Information gathering (reconnaissance):**

   - Passive reconnaissance: Collect information without directly interacting with the target, such as through public sources or social media. Passive reconnaissance uses open-source intelligence (OSINT) techniques to gather publicly available information that can assist in later phases.

   - Active reconnaissance: Gather information by directly interacting with the target, using techniques such as DNS queries, network scanning, and WHOIS searches.

3. **Threat modeling:**

   - Analyze and prioritize potential threats and vulnerabilities based on the gathered information.

   - Determine the potential impact and likelihood of successful exploitation for each identified threat.

4. **Vulnerability analysis:**

   - Identify and assess vulnerabilities in the target system or application.

   - Use tools and manual testing to discover weaknesses in security controls.

5. **Exploitation:**

   - Attempt to exploit identified vulnerabilities to validate their existence and assess the severity.

   - Simulate real-world attack scenarios to understand the potential impact on the system.

6. **Post-exploitation:**

   - Examine the consequences of successful exploitation, such as access gained, data compromised, or achieved system control.

   - Assess the ability to maintain persistence within the target environment.

7. **Reporting:**

   - Document findings in a detailed report, including a summary of the penetration test, the identified vulnerabilities and their severity, and recommended remediation steps.

   - Provide clear and actionable recommendations for improving security.

8. **Debriefing:**

   - Discuss with stakeholders to review the results, answer questions, and address concerns.

   - Share insights into the system's security posture and discuss potential mitigation strategies.

9. **Remediation verification:**

   - Confirm that the identified vulnerabilities have been remediated by retesting the affected areas.

   - Ensure that the recommended security controls are effectively implemented.

10. **Continuous monitoring and improvement:**

    - Implement continuous monitoring practices to detect new vulnerabilities or changes in the security landscape.

    - Learn from the penetration testing experience and use the insights to improve security practices.

It's worth noting that penetration testing is an iterative process, and organizations may conduct tests regularly to stay ahead of evolving threats and changes in their systems. Adherence to ethical guidelines and legal considerations is also crucial throughout the penetration testing process. For example, in our running example of the ticketing software, many organizations perform a vulnerability scan nightly for any public interface (web applications, mobile applications, kiosks, etc.) to ensure any new vulnerability knowledge is applied quickly and the problems are fixed before they can be exploited.

Tools

Penetration testing tools are essential for security professionals to identify vulnerabilities and assess the security of software, networks, and systems. Here are some commonly used penetration testing tools, categorized based on their functionalities.

Information gathering and reconnaissance

Information gathering and reconnaissance are critical phases of cybersecurity and penetration testing. These phases involve collecting data about the target system, network, or organization to gain insights into potential vulnerabilities, weaknesses, and attack vectors:

- **Nmap** (network mapper): Nmap is a powerful open source scanning tool for network discovery and security auditing. It allows users to discover hosts and services on a computer network, thus creating a network map. Nmap utilizes the raw IP packets to determine which hosts are visible on the network, what services those hosts offer, what operating systems they are running, what type of firewalls are in use, and other attributes. *Figure 14.1* shows a screenshot of the command line use of Nmap:

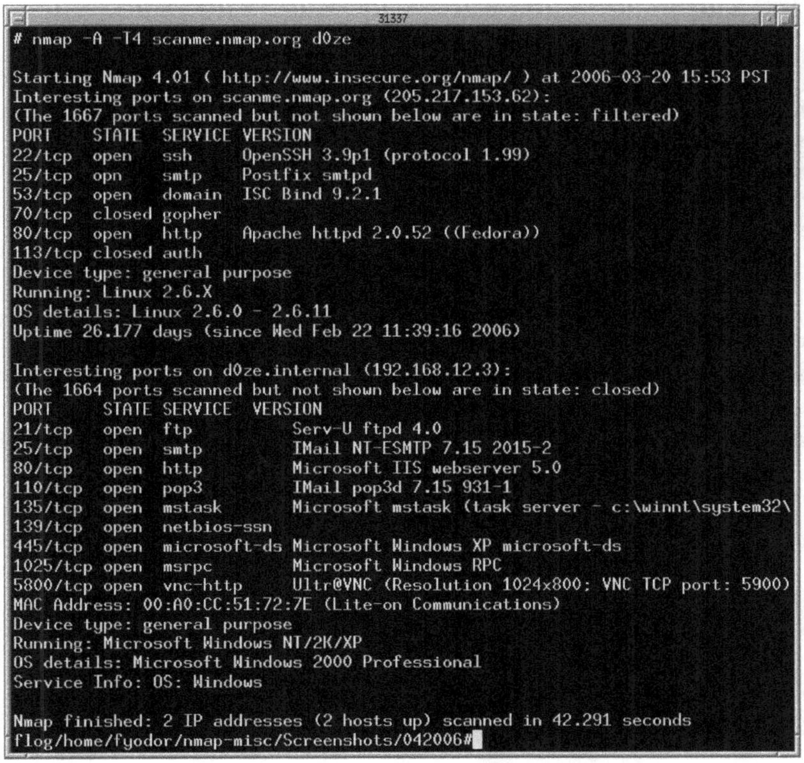

Figure 14.1 – Command line use for NMap

- **Maltego**: Maltego is a powerful data visualization and analysis tool for gathering and correlating information about people, organizations, and relationships from various online sources. It allows users to perform link analysis, network reconnaissance, and OSINT gathering to facilitate investigations and intelligence gathering. *Figure 14.2* shows a screenshot of information Maltego was able to obtain for the gnu.org domain:

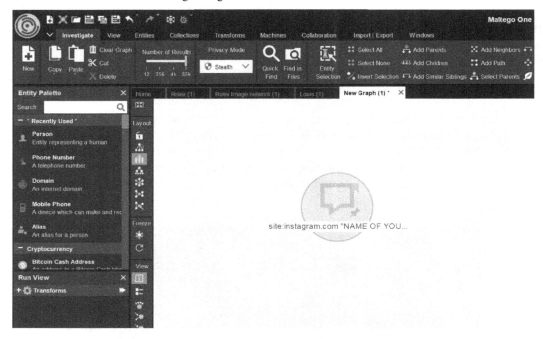

Figure 14.2 – Maltego display of open source intelligence

- **theHarvester**: theHarvester is an OSINT tool used for gathering information about email addresses, domain names, and subdomains from various public sources on the internet. It's commonly used by security professionals, penetration testers, and investigators to conduct reconnaissance and gather intelligence during security assessments and investigations. *Figure 14.3* shows a screenshot of theHarvester command line interface:

```
root@kali:~# theharvester

*******************************************************************
*                                                                 *
*  | |_| |__   ___    /\  /\__ _ _ ____   _____  ___| |_ ___ _ __  *
*  | __| '_ \ / _ \  / /_/ / _` | '__\ \ / / _ \/ __| __/ _ \ '__| *
*  | |_| | | |  __/ / __  / (_| | |   \ V /  __/\__ \ ||  __/ |    *
*   \__|_| |_|\___| \/ /_/ \__,_|_|    \_/ \___||___/\__\___|_|    *
*                                                                 *
* TheHarvester Ver. 2.7                                           *
* Coded by Christian Martorella                                   *
* Edge-Security Research                                          *
* cmartorella@edge-security.com                                   *
*******************************************************************


Usage: theharvester options

       -d: Domain to search or company name
       -b: data source: google, googleCSE, exalead, bing, bingapi, pgp, linkedin,
                        google-profiles, jigsaw, twitter, googleplus, all

       -s: Start in result number X (default: 0)
       -v: Verify host name via dns resolution and search for virtual hosts
       -f: Save the results into an HTML and XML file (both)
       -n: Perform a DNS reverse query on all ranges discovered
       -c: Perform a DNS brute force for the domain name
       -t: Perform a DNS TLD expansion discovery
       -e: Use this DNS server
       -l: Limit the number of results to work with(bing goes from 50 to 50 results,
           google 100 to 100, and pgp doesn't use this option)
       -h: use SHODAN database to query discovered hosts

Examples:
        theharvester -d microsoft.com -l 500 -b google -f myresults.html
        theharvester -d microsoft.com -b pgp
        theharvester -d microsoft -l 200 -b linkedin
        theharvester -d apple.com -b googleCSE -l 500 -s 300
```

Figure 14.3 – theHarvester command line

Vulnerability analysis and exploitation

Vulnerability analysis and exploitation are critical phases of cybersecurity and penetration testing. These phases involve identifying and exploiting security vulnerabilities and weaknesses in target systems, networks, or applications:

- **Metasploit**: Metasploit is a popular penetration testing framework enabling security professionals to assess and exploit the vulnerabilities of computer systems, networks, and applications. It provides a comprehensive suite of tools for penetration testing, including exploit development, payload generation, post-exploitation modules, and social engineering attacks. Metasploit is widely used by security researchers, penetration testers, and ethical hackers to identify and remediate security weaknesses in target systems. *Figure 14.4* shows a screenshot of the Metasploit command line:

```
        .:ok000kdc'            'cdk000ko:.
      .x00000000000c          c00000000000x.
     :000000000000000k,      ,k000000000000000:
    '000000000kkkk00000: :00000000000000000000'
    o00000000.MMMM.00000o00000l.MMMM,000000000o
    d00000000.MMMMMMM.c00000c.MMMMMMM,00000000C.x
    l00000000.MMMMMMMMM;d;MMMMMMMMMM,00000000C0l
    .00000000.MMM.;MMMMMMMMMMM;MMMM,00000000U.
    c0000000.MMM.00c.MMMMM'000.MMM,0000000C
     o000000.MMM.0000.MMM'0000.MMM,0000000o
      l00000.MMM.0000.MMM'0000.MMM,00000l
      ;0000'MMM.0000.MMM'0000.MMM'0000;
      .d00o'WM.0000cccx0000.MX'x00d.
       ,k0!'M.0000000000000.M'd0k,
        :kk;.0000000000000.;0k:
          ;k00000000000000k:
            ,x00000000000x,
              .l0000000l.
                ,d0d,


         =[ metasploit v6.1.14-dev               ]
  + -- --=[ 2180 exploits - 1155 auxiliary - 399 post  ]
  + -- --=[ 592 payloads - 45 encoders - 10 nops        ]
  + -- --=[ 9 evasion                                    ]

Metasploit tip: Open an interactive Ruby terminal with
irb

msf6 >
```

Figure 14.4 – Metasploit command line

- **Nessus**: Nessus is a widely-used vulnerability scanning tool developed by Tenable network security. It is designed to scan computer networks for vulnerabilities, misconfigurations, and security weaknesses, providing detailed reports that help organizations identify and prioritize security issues. Figure 14.5 shows a screenshot of the Nessus scanner web application:

Figure 14.5 – Nessus web app scan templates

- **Burp Suite**: Burp Suite is a web application penetration testing platform. PortSwigger developed Burp Suite, which is widely used by security professionals, penetration testers, and web developers to find and mitigate security vulnerabilities in web applications. *Figure 14.6* shows a screenshot of the Burp Suite application:

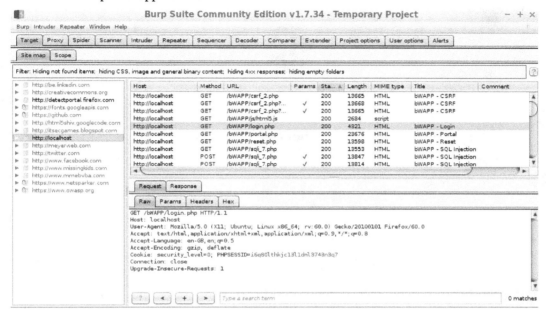

Figure 14.6 – Burp Suite proxy capture

- **VEGA**: Vega is an open source web vulnerability scanner and testing platform used by security professionals, penetration testers, and web developers to identify and remediate security vulnerabilities in web applications. It provides a user-friendly graphical interface and tools for automated scanning, manual testing, and vulnerability analysis. *Figure 14.7* shows a screenshot of the Vega scanner:

Figure 14.7 - The Vega Scanner

- **OWASP ZAP** (Zed Attack Proxy): OWASP ZAP is a web application security testing tool developed by the Open Web Application Security Project (OWASP). It is designed to help users identify and mitigate security vulnerabilities in web applications. OWASP ZAP is open source and free for anyone to use. Figure 14.8 shows a screenshot of OWASP Zap:

Figure 14.8 – OWASP Zap home screen

- **SQLmap:** SQLmap is a database penetration testing tool that automates detecting and exploiting SQL injection vulnerabilities in web applications. It allows the user to identify and exploit SQL injection flaws in a target application's database backend. *Figure 14.9* shows the results of an SQLMap scan against a database:

```
$ python sqlmap.py -u "http://debiandev/sqlmap/mysql/get_int.php?id=1" --batch
                        {1.0.5.63#dev}
|_ -| . ["]     | .'| . |
|___|_  [,]_|_|_|__,|  _|
      |_|V          |_|   http://sqlmap.org

[!] legal disclaimer: Usage of sqlmap for attacking targets without prior mutual consent i
s illegal. It is the end user's responsibility to obey all applicable local, state and fed
eral laws. Developers assume no liability and are not responsible for any misuse or damage
caused by this program

[*] starting at 17:43:06

[17:43:06] [INFO] testing connection to the target URL
[17:43:06] [INFO] heuristics detected web page charset 'ascii'
[17:43:06] [INFO] testing if the target URL is stable
[17:43:07] [INFO] target URL is stable
[17:43:07] [INFO] testing if GET parameter 'id' is dynamic
[17:43:07] [INFO] confirming that GET parameter 'id' is dynamic
[17:43:07] [INFO] GET parameter 'id' is dynamic
[17:43:07] [INFO] heuristic (basic) test shows that GET parameter 'id' might be injectable
(possible DBMS: 'MySQL')
```

Figure 14.9 – SQLMap scan

Post-exploitation and privilege escalation

Post-exploitation and privilege escalation are critical phases in the cybersecurity and penetration testing processes, typically occurring after initial access has been gained to a target system or network. During these phases, attackers aim to extend their control over the compromised environment, escalate their privileges, and maintain persistent access for future exploitation.

- **PowerShell Empire**: PowerShell Empire is a post-exploitation framework designed for red team operations and penetration testing. It provides powerful tools and modules for maintaining persistence, escalating privileges, and exfiltrating data on compromised Windows systems. PowerShell Empire is often used by security professionals, penetration testers, and red teamers to simulate advanced persistent threat (APT) attacks and assess an organization's security posture. *Figure 14.10* shows a screenshot of Power Shell Empire:

Figure 14.10 – Powershell Empire

- **Mimikatz**: Mimikatz is a powerful post-exploitation tool that is commonly used by security professionals, penetration testers, and attackers to extract plaintext passwords, hashes, and Kerberos tickets from computer memory on Windows systems. Developed by Benjamin Delpy, Mimikatz has become widely known for its ability to perform credential theft and pass-the-hash attacks, among other post-exploitation activities. *Figure 14.11* shows a screenshot of Mimkatz password extraction:

```
 .#####.    mimikatz 2.2.0 (x64) #17763 Apr  10 2019 00:55
 .## ^ ##.  "A La Vie, A L'Amour" - (oe.eo)
 ## / \ ##  /*** Benjamin DELPY gentilkiwi ( benjamin@gentilkiwi.com )
 ## \ / ##       > http://blog.gentilkiwi.com/mimikatz
 '## v ##'       Vincent LE TOUX            ( vincent.letoux@gmail.com )
  '#####'        > http://pingcastle.com / http://mysmartlogon.com   ***/

mimikatz # privilege::debug
privilege '20' OK

mimikatz # sekurlsa::logonpasswords

Authentication Id : 0 ; 234764 (00000000:0002deb6)
Session           : Interactive from 2
User Name         : user
Domain            : test-PC-x64
SID               : S-1-5-21-1982681256-1210654043-1600862990-1000
        msv :
         [00000003] Primary
         * Username : test
         * Domain   : test-PC-x64
         * LM       : d0e9aee149655a6075e4540af1f22d3b
         * NTLM     : cc36cf7a8514893efccd332446158b1a
         * SHA1     : a299912f3dc7cf0023aef8e4361abfc03e9a8c30
        tspkg :
         * Username : user
         * Domain   : test-PC-x64
         * Password : t3stus3r
...
```

Figure 14.11 – Mimikatz command line interface

Network sniffing

Network Sniffing tools are usually used for infrastructure penetration testing, not software penetration testing, but can be helpful in understanding vulnerabilities in the data that a user's software passes over the network.

- **Aircrack-ng**: Aircrack-ng is a popular suite of tools used for testing and analyzing the security of wireless networks. It is widely used by security professionals, penetration testers, and network administrators to assess the vulnerabilities of Wi-Fi networks and to conduct wireless security audits. *Figure 14.12* shows a screenshot of Aircrack-ng cracking WiFi-passwords:

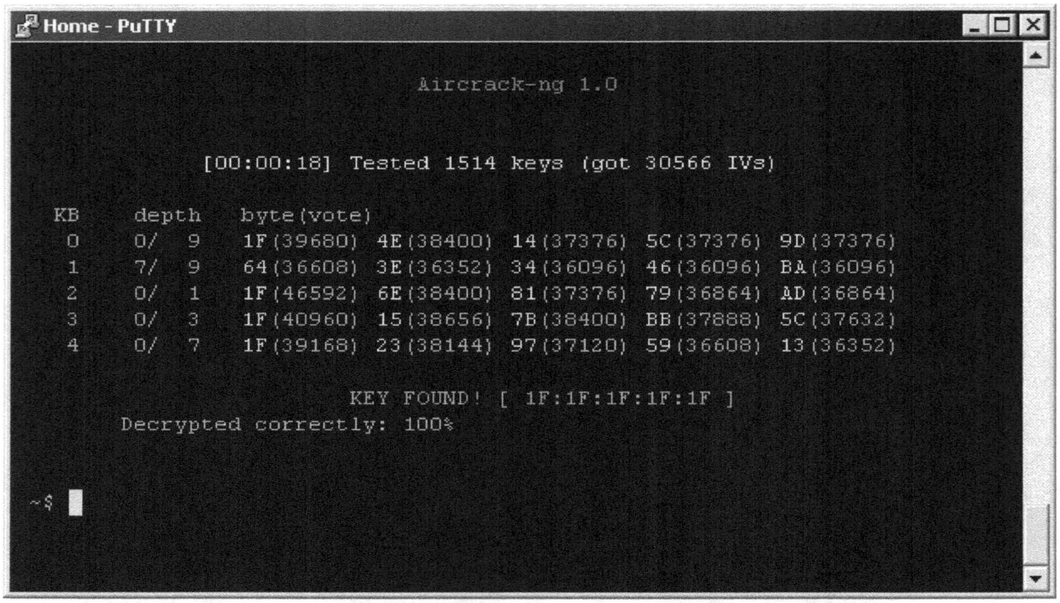

Figure 14.12 – Aircrack-ng password cracking

- **Wireshark:** Wireshark is a powerful network protocol analyzer and packet capture tool used by network administrators, security professionals, developers, and educators to capture, analyze, and troubleshoot network traffic in real time. It allows users to inspect the data packets flowing through a network interface or saved in a packet capture file. Wireshark is a great tool to see what data your application sends and whether it can be deciphered. *Figure 14.13* shows a capture of network traffic in Wireshark:

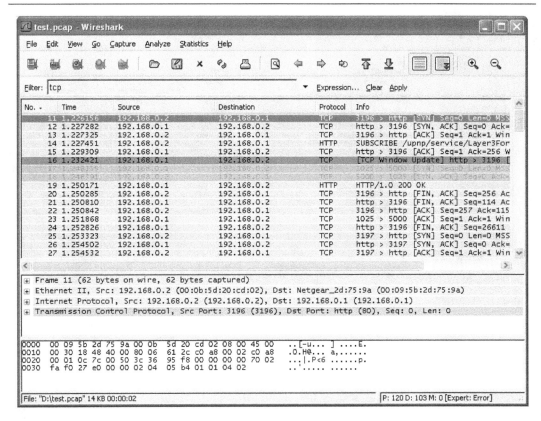

Figure 14.13 – Wireshark capture screen

Forensics and monitoring

In penetration testing, forensics and monitoring play essential roles in understanding the impact of security assessments, identifying potential risks, and ensuring that penetration testing activities are conducted responsibly and ethically:

- **Autopsy**: Autopsy is an open source digital forensics platform used by forensic examiners, law enforcement agencies, and cybersecurity professionals to analyze and investigate digital evidence collected from computers, storage devices, and mobile devices. It provides a comprehensive set of tools for conducting forensic analysis, including file system analysis, keyword search, timeline analysis, and artifact examination. *Figure 14.14* shows a screenshot of the case management screen in Autopsy:

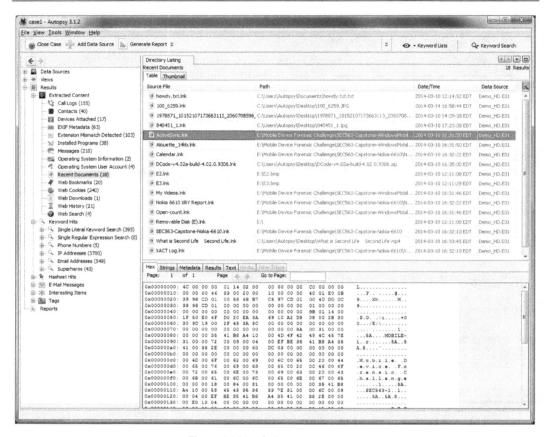

Figure 14.14 – Autopsy case screen

- **Snort**: Snort is an open source network intrusion detection and prevention system (NIDS/NIPS) developed by Sourcefire that is now owned by Cisco. It is widely used by security professionals, network administrators, and organizations to detect and prevent malicious network traffic and attacks in real time. *Figure 14.15* shows a screenshot of an alert in the Snort IDS:

```
[**] [1:100006927:1] SSH incoming [**]
[Priority: 0]
05/24-17:07:32.944415 192.168.0.105:37024 -> 192.168.0.103:22
TCP TTL:64 TOS:0x0 ID:23182 IpLen:20 DgmLen:60 DF
******S* Seq: 0xA014F9DA  Ack: 0x0  Win: 0xFAF0  TcpLen: 40
TCP Options (5) => MSS: 1460 SackOK TS: 3936797066 0 NOP WS: 7

[**] [1:1418:11] SNMP request tcp [**]
[Classification: Attempted Information Leak] [Priority: 2]
05/24-17:07:33.957372 192.168.0.105:58280 -> 192.168.0.103:161
TCP TTL:64 TOS:0x0 ID:38305 IpLen:20 DgmLen:60 DF
******S* Seq: 0xD43018E8  Ack: 0x0  Win: 0xFAF0  TcpLen: 40
TCP Options (5) => MSS: 1460 SackOK TS: 3936798079 0 NOP WS: 7
[Xref => http://cve.mitre.org/cgi-bin/cvename.cgi?name=2002-0013][Xref =>
http://cve.mitre.org/cgi-bin/cvename.cgi?name=2002-0012][Xref => http://ww
w.securityfocus.com/bid/4132][Xref => http://www.securityfocus.com/bid/408
9][Xref => http://www.securityfocus.com/bid/4088]
:
```

Figure 14.15 – Snort alert notification

Reporting and documentation

Reporting and documentation are crucial aspects of penetration testing as they effectively communicate the findings, vulnerabilities, and recommendations to stakeholders. A well-written and comprehensive report helps organizations understand their security posture, prioritize remediation efforts, and improve their security resilience.

- **Dradis framework**: The Dradis framework is an open source collaboration and reporting platform designed to facilitate the sharing, integration, and management of information generated during security assessments and penetration testing engagements. It streamlines documenting findings, organizing evidence, and generating professional-looking reports, helping security professionals and teams deliver more efficient and consistent results. *Figure 14.16* shows the dashboard of a project in the Dradis framework:

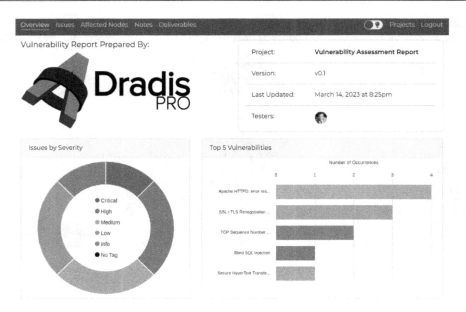

Figure 14.16 – Dradis dashboard view

- **Faraday**: Faraday is an open source collaborative security platform designed to facilitate the management of information and workflows during penetration testing, vulnerability assessment, and incident response processes. It provides a centralized environment for security teams to collaborate, organize findings, track progress, and generate reports efficiently. *Figure 14.17* shows the dashboard of a project in Faraday:

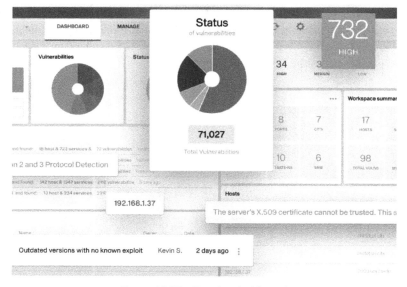

Figure 14.17 – Faraday dashboard

These tools should be used responsibly and ethically. Always ensure you have proper authorization before conducting penetration testing activities and be aware of legal and ethical considerations. Additionally, the effectiveness of penetration testing often relies on a combination of automated tools and manual testing by skilled security professionals. There are Linux distributions, such as Kali Linux, that include many tools that the security professional needs and that we have mentioned here.

An example of an enterprise penetration test report

Throughout this book, we will build a secure design for an event ticketing system. Envision a software system that allows a box office or a website to sell tickets to a famous musical concert or theatre event. A simplified sample penetration test report is detailed in the following:

High-level summary

A workstation, web server, and database server were analyzed. The workstations were found to be vulnerable if malware was installed. The malware may be able to modify and read the API calls. The web server had some common web vulnerabilities, which are included in the Vega report. The database server had a single potential SQL injection vulnerability. The recommendations are included in the following individual host analysis section. Periodic scanning of the web and database servers is included in the recommendations.

Host analysis

This section of the report will document the reconnaissance, vulnerability analysis, exploitation, and recommendations for machines involved in the penetration testing:

Web server

Reconnaissance

- Tool used: NMap
- IP address: 192.168.1.1
- Subnet: 255.255.255.0
- MAC address: 00-A5-B1-65-C2-32
- Operating system: RHEL 9
- Other software discovered: Apache, PHP

Vulnerability analysis

- Tools used: Vega

- Many vulnerabilities were discovered when utilizing Vega; see the attached listing. The examples include the following:

  - XSS in ticketbasket.php

  - SQL injection in ticketpayment.php

Exploitation

- An XSS attack was developed and delivered against the ticketbasket.php page

> **Important note**
>
> We discussed XSS attacks in *Chapter 9, Standard Web Application Vulnerabilities.*

Recommendations

- Fix all attached vulnerabilities and run a Vega scan nightly.

Database server

Reconnaissance

- Tool used: NMap
- IP address: 192.168.1.121
- Subnet: 255.255.255.0
- MAC address: 00-E5-B1-23-A2-54
- Operating system: RHEL 9
- API connectivity: MySQL API
- Other software discovered: MySQL 8.2

Vulnerability analysis

- Tools used: SQLMap
- Potential SQL injection in the stored procedure: spLockSeats

> **Important note**
>
> We discuss this type of vulnerability and mitigations in *Chapter 10, Database Security.*

Exploitation

- SQLMap was utilized to attempt exploitation without success.

Recommendations

- Fix the stored procedure and run an Nmap scan against a backup server weekly.

Bos office workstation

Reconnaissance

- Tool used: NMap
- IP address: 192.168.1.120
- Subnet: 255.255.255.0
- MAC address: 00-F5-A1-63-D2-52
- Operating system: Windows 11
- API connectivity: REST
- Other software discovered: MS Teams, MS RDP

Vulnerability analysis

- Tools used: Burp Suite
- Malware can modify HTTPS requests to REST API

> **Important note**
> We did not directly discuss this, but it is part of the input sanitization and validation in *Chapter 8*.

Exploitation

- A malware was developed and deployed that mutated the REST calls to cause a denial of service in the application.

Recommendations

- Use X.509 client certificates

Summary

This chapter introduces penetration testing. We looked at types of penetration tests and the phases of penetration testing. Next, we looked at the tools that are helpful in the different phases of penetration testing. We concluded with a simple example penetration test for our book-wide example application.

Self-assessment questions

1. Which of the following best describes software penetration testing?

    A. Verifying software's compliance with industry standards and regulations

    B. Testing software for performance and scalability issues

    C. Evaluating a piece of software's user interface and user experience

    D. Assessing a piece of software's security by attempting to exploit vulnerabilities

2. What is the primary goal of penetration testing?

    A. To ensure the software meets user requirements

    B. To uncover security weaknesses and vulnerabilities in the software

    C. To verify the software's functionality across different platforms

    D. To identify all bugs and defects in the software

3. Which of the following types of penetration testing simulates a real-world cyberattack by attempting to exploit vulnerabilities without prior knowledge of the system?

    A. Gray-box testing

    B. Fuzz testing

    C. White-box testing

    D. Black-box testing

4. Which phase of penetration testing involves planning, gathering information about the target system, and defining the scope and objectives of the test?

    A. Reporting

    B. Reconnaissance

    C. Analysis

    D. Exploitation

5. What is the difference between vulnerability scanning and penetration testing?

   A. Vulnerability scanning identifies security weaknesses, whereas penetration testing exploits them

   B. Vulnerability scanning attempts to bypass security controls, whereas penetration testing identifies misconfigurations

   C. Vulnerability scanning is automated, whereas penetration testing requires manual intervention

   D. Vulnerability scanning focuses on software functionality, whereas penetration testing focuses on user experience

Answers

   1. D
   2. B
   3. D
   4. B
   5. A

Index

packtpub.com

Subscribe to our online digital library for full access to over 7,000 books and videos, as well as industry leading tools to help you plan your personal development and advance your career. For more information, please visit our website.

Why subscribe?

- Spend less time learning and more time coding with practical eBooks and Videos from over 4,000 industry professionals
- Improve your learning with Skill Plans built especially for you
- Get a free eBook or video every month
- Fully searchable for easy access to vital information
- Copy and paste, print, and bookmark content

Did you know that Packt offers eBook versions of every book published, with PDF and ePub files available? You can upgrade to the eBook version at packtpub.com and as a print book customer, you are entitled to a discount on the eBook copy. Get in touch with us at customercare@packtpub.com for more details.

At www.packtpub.com, you can also read a collection of free technical articles, sign up for a range of free newsletters, and receive exclusive discounts and offers on Packt books and eBooks.

Other Books You May Enjoy

If you enjoyed this book, you may be interested in these other books by Packt:

Expert C++

Marcelo Guerra Hahn, Araks Tigranyan, John Asatryan, Vardan Grigoryan, Shunguang Wu

ISBN: 978-1-80461-783-0

- Go beyond the basics to explore advanced C++ programming techniques
- Develop proficiency in advanced data structures and algorithm design with C++17 and C++20
- Implement best practices and design patterns to build scalable C++ applications
- Master C++ for machine learning, data science, and data analysis framework design
- Design world-ready applications, incorporating networking and security considerations
- Strengthen your understanding of C++ concurrency, multithreading, and optimizing performance with concurrent data structures

Developer Career Masterplan

Heather VanCura, Bruno Souza

ISBN: 978-1-80181-870-4

- Explore skills needed to grow your career
- Participate in community and mentorship programs
- Build your technical knowledge for growth
- Discover how to network and use social media
- Understand the impact of public speaking
- Identify the critical conversations to advance your career
- Participate in non-technical activities to enhance your career

Packt is searching for authors like you

If you're interested in becoming an author for Packt, please visit `authors.packtpub.com` and apply today. We have worked with thousands of developers and tech professionals, just like you, to help them share their insight with the global tech community. You can make a general application, apply for a specific hot topic that we are recruiting an author for, or submit your own idea.

Share your thoughts

Now you've finished *Security-Driven Software Development*, we'd love to hear your thoughts! Scan the QR code below to go straight to the Amazon review page for this book and share your feedback or leave a review on the site that you purchased it from.

`https://packt.link/r/1835462839`

Your review is important to us and the tech community and will help us make sure we're delivering excellent quality content.

Download a free PDF copy of this book

Thanks for purchasing this book!

Do you like to read on the go but are unable to carry your print books everywhere?

Is your eBook purchase not compatible with the device of your choice?

Don't worry, now with every Packt book you get a DRM-free PDF version of that book at no cost.

Read anywhere, any place, on any device. Search, copy, and paste code from your favorite technical books directly into your application.

The perks don't stop there, you can get exclusive access to discounts, newsletters, and great free content in your inbox daily

Follow these simple steps to get the benefits:

1. Scan the QR code or visit the link below

https://packt.link/free-ebook/9781835462836

2. Submit your proof of purchase

3. That's it! We'll send your free PDF and other benefits to your email directly

www.ingramcontent.com/pod-product-compliance
Lightning Source LLC
Chambersburg PA
CBHW080634060326
40690CB00021B/4932